MathFlare

Name: ______________________

Class: ___________

Teacher: ______________________

Introduction

As parents and educators, we recognize the pivotal role mathematics plays in shaping a child's academic journey and future success. Yet, the path to mathematical proficiency can often seem daunting, fraught with challenges and complexities. That's where the transformative power of MathFlare Workbooks shine through, illuminating the way forward with clarity, precision, and purpose.

Introducing MathFlare Workbooks – a beacon of guidance, a testament to excellence, and a catalyst for achievement. Crafted with meticulous care and expertise, MathFlare Workbooks stand as paragons of educational excellence, designed to nurture young minds, ignite a passion for learning, and develop a deep-rooted understanding of mathematical concepts.

Picture this: your child eagerly delves into the pages of Mathflare Workbook, greeted by a step-by-step guide illuminated with vivid examples that demystify complex mathematical concepts. With each turn of the page, they embark on a journey of discovery, encountering thoughtfully curated practice questions that reinforce learning and hone problem-solving skills. And when they unveil the answers to those very questions, a sense of accomplishment blossoms within them – a tangible reward for their hard work and dedication.

But MathFlare Workbooks are more than just tools for learning; they are pathways to comprehension, fostering a deep-seated understanding of mathematical concepts through a sequential, logical flow. From fundamental principles to advanced problem-solving strategies, every chapter builds upon the last, ensuring a robust foundation upon which future knowledge can be constructed.

As parents, we yearn for nothing more than to see our children thrive, to witness the spark of inspiration ignited within them as they conquer academic challenges with confidence and poise. MathFlare Workbooks serve as partners in this noble endeavor, offering not just practice questions, but the keys to unlocking a world of opportunity.

And for teachers, MathFlare Workbooks stand as invaluable allies in the quest to cultivate mathematical proficiency in the classroom. With answers readily available, instructors can focus on guiding and nurturing their students, confident in the knowledge that MathFlare Workbooks provide a solid framework upon which to build.

In the pages of MathFlare Workbooks, we find not just the promise of academic excellence, but the seeds of a brighter tomorrow. So let us embrace the power of mathematics, let us champion the journey of learning, and let us pave the way for a generation of young minds poised to shape the world. With MathFlare Workbooks as our guide, the possibilities are infinite, and the future, bright.

Table of Contents

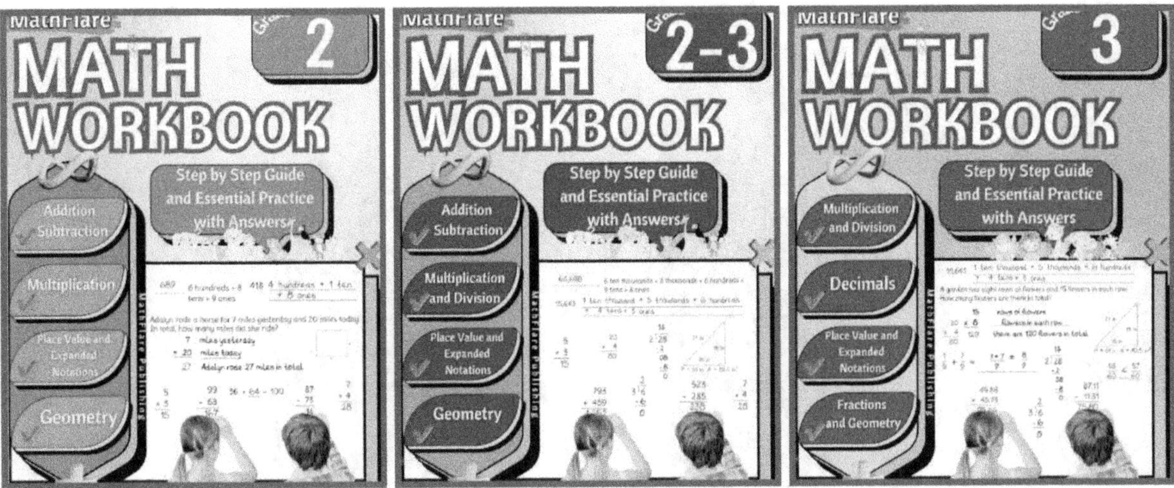

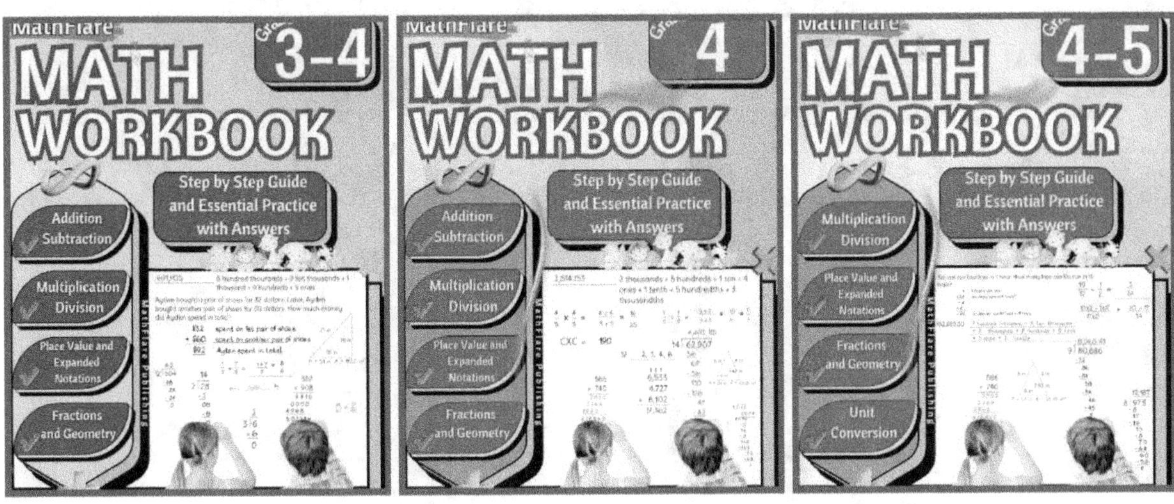

MathFlare
MATH
WORKBOOK
Grade 5
Step by Step Guide
and Essential Practice
with Answers
Multiplication Division
Place Value and Expanded Notations
Fractions and Geometry
Unit Conversion
MathFlare Publishing

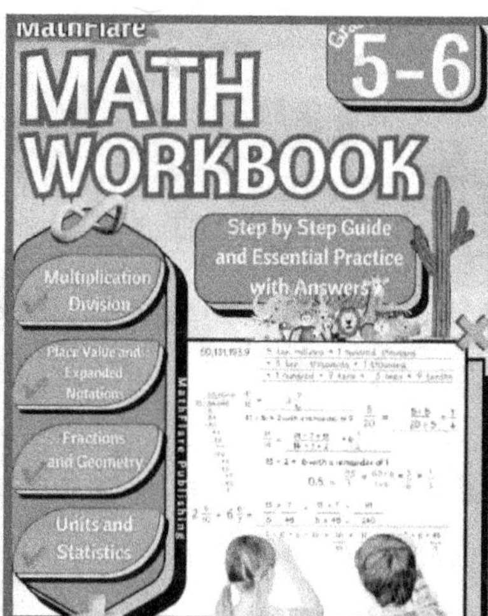
MathFlare
MATH
WORKBOOK
Grade 5-6
Step by Step Guide
and Essential Practice
with Answers
Multiplication Division
Place Value and Expanded Notations
Fractions and Geometry
Units and Statistics
MathFlare Publishing

MathFlare
MATH
WORKBOOK
Grade 6
Step by Step Guide
and Essential Practice
with Answers
Integers and Statistics
Arithmetic and Pre-Algebra
Fractions and Geometry
Ratio and Percentage
MathFlare Publishing

MathFlare
MATH
WORKBOOK
Grade 6-7
Step by Step Guide
and Essential Practice
with Answers
Arithmetic and Pre-Algebra
Ratio, Percent Proportion
Geometry
Statistics
MathFlare Publishing

MathFlare
MATH
WORKBOOK
Grade 7
Step by Step Guide
and Essential Practice
with Answers
Pre-Algebra
Ratio, Percent Proportion
Geometry
Statistics
MathFlare Publishing

MathFlare
MATH
WORKBOOK
Grade 7-8
Step by Step Guide
and Essential Practice
with Answers
Pre-Algebra
Ratio, Percent Proportion
Geometry and Cartesian Plane
Statistics
MathFlare Publishing

MathFlare
MATH
WORKBOOK
Grade 8-9
Step by Step Guide
and Essential Practice
with Answers
Pre-Algebra
Ratio, Proportion and Percentage
Linear Equations
Geometry and Cartesian Plane
MathFlare Publishing

MathFlare
MATH
WORKBOOK
Grade 8
Step by Step Guide
and Essential Practice
with Answers
Pre-Algebra
Percentage
Linear Equations
Geometry
MathFlare Publishing

Addition and Subtraction

Addition with Regrouping

When we do addition, we combine numbers. But sometimes, when we're adding numbers, we might need to regroup. Regrouping means we must move a number from one place to another, usually to the next column, to get the right answer.

For Example: Let's take an example of adding 33 and 79 together:

```
   3 3
 + 7 9
```

First, we start by adding the digits in the ones place: 3 + 9 = 12. We write down the 2 in the ones place and carry over the 1 to the tens place.

```
   1
   3 3
 + 7 9
     2
```

Now, we add the digits in the tens place, along with the carry-over: 3 + 7 + 1 = 11. We write down the 1 in the tens place and carry over the 1 to the hundreds place.

```
   1
   2 2
 + 8 9
   1 1 1
```

This process of carrying over helps us accurately add numbers, especially when they're larger.

Subtraction with Regrouping

Subtraction is a key math operation where we find the difference between two numbers. Sometimes, when we subtract, we might need to regroup, which means borrowing from the next column.

Let's take an example of subtracting 36 from 63:

First, we start by subtracting the digits in the ones place: 3 - 6. Since 3 is less than 6, we need to regroup. We borrow 1 from the tens place, making it 5 tens instead of 6, and add it to the ones place.

So, 3 becomes 13, and then we subtract 6.

$$
\begin{array}{r}
6\ 13 \\
-\ 3\ 6 \\
\hline
7
\end{array}
$$

Now, we subtract the tens place digits: 5 - 3 = 2

$$
\begin{array}{r}
5 \\
\cancel{6}\ 13 \\
-\ 3\ 6 \\
\hline
2\ 7
\end{array}
$$

This process of regrouping or borrowing helps us accurately subtract numbers, especially when the top digit is smaller than the bottom one.

Let's solve problems from the exercises:

$$
\begin{array}{r}
99 \\
+\ 68 \\
\hline
167
\end{array}
\qquad
\begin{array}{r}
33 \\
-\ 28 \\
\hline
5
\end{array}
$$

Addition and Subtraction: Unknown Numbers

When we have a situation where we need to find the missing number in an equation, we're usually solving for an unknown.

In this case, we have the equation 20−___=12.

We're trying to figure out what number we need to subtract from 20 to get 12.

We know that 20−___=12, so we can subtract 12 from 20:

$$20 - 12 = 8$$

Let's solve problems from exercises:

$$63 + \underline{\ 37\ } = 100$$

$$25 - \underline{\ 20\ } = 5$$

Word Problems

Word problems are like little puzzles that help us use addition in real-life situations.

For instance:

1. Jake has 6 carrots. He gets 2 more carrots. How many carrots does he have now?

To find out how many carrots he has now, we add the number of carrots he started with (6) to the number of carrots he got (2).

So, we add 6 + 2, which equals 8.

Jake now has 8 carrots in total!

2. Jake saved up 4 dollars to buy pencils. He spent 2 dollars on it. How much money does he have left?

To solve this problem, we need to start with the number of dollars Jake started with and subtract the number of dollars he spent on the pencils.

So, we subtract 2 from 4, which equals 2:

Jake has 2 dollars left after buying the pencils.

We need to understand what the problem is asking and what information it provides. Then, we can use addition or subtraction, depending on whether we're combining or taking away objects, to find the answer.

Let's solve problems from exercises:

Adalyn rode a horse for 7 miles yesterday and 20 miles today. In total, how many miles did she ride?

$$
\begin{array}{rl}
7 & \text{miles yesterday} \\
+\ 20 & \text{miles today} \\
\hline
27 & \text{Adalyn rode 27 miles in total}
\end{array}
$$

Emma and Sharon had 5 maps altogether. Sharon gave 3 maps   to Billy. How many maps do they have left?

$$
\begin{array}{rl}
5 & \text{Emma and Sharon have 5 maps} \\
-\ 3 & \text{Sharon Gave 3 maps to Billy} \\
\hline
2 & \text{they have 2 maps left}
\end{array}
$$

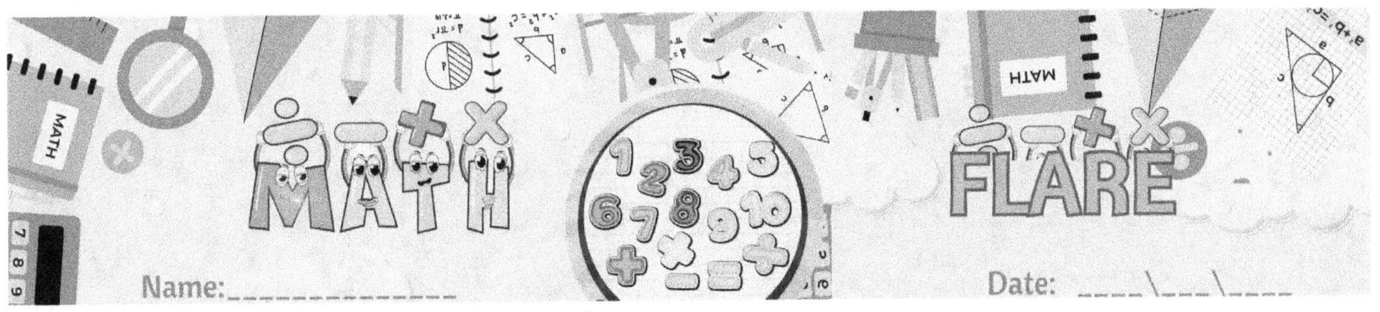

Addition: 1 through 100

Find the Sum.

1. 52 + 48	2. 35 + 83	3. 56 + 63	4. 5 + 6
5. 57 + 71	6. 53 + 84	7. 83 + 80	8. 14 + 30
9. 35 + 42	10. 71 + 9	11. 86 + 63	12. 2 + 54
13. 69 + 10	14. 51 + 9	15. 51 + 43	16. 36 + 68

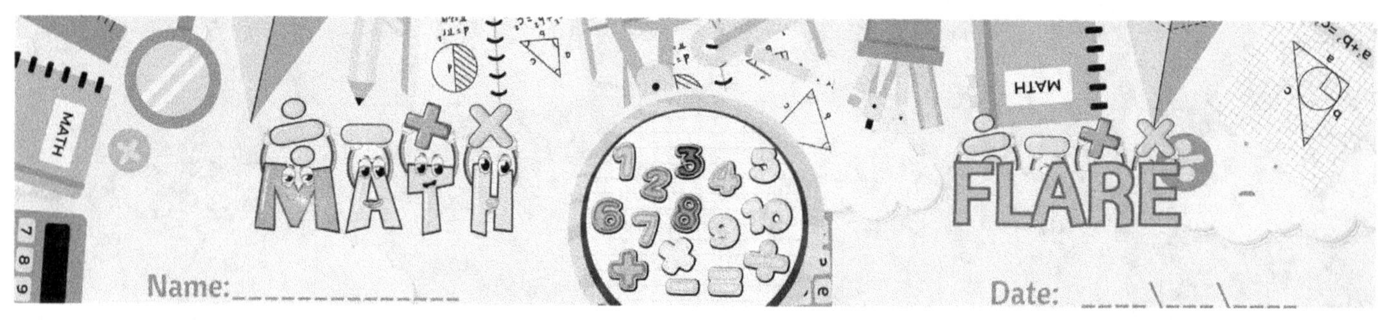

17. 44 + 75	18. 50 + 35	19. 14 + 34	20. 19 + 22
21. 75 + 30	22. 96 + 78	23. 65 + 31	24. 69 + 71
25. 38 + 64	26. 79 + 28	27. 47 + 78	28. 22 + 89
29. 47 + 81	30. 15 + 47	31. 13 + 96	32. 56 + 14
33. 36 + 84	34. 41 + 9	35. 31 + 79	36. 17 + 2

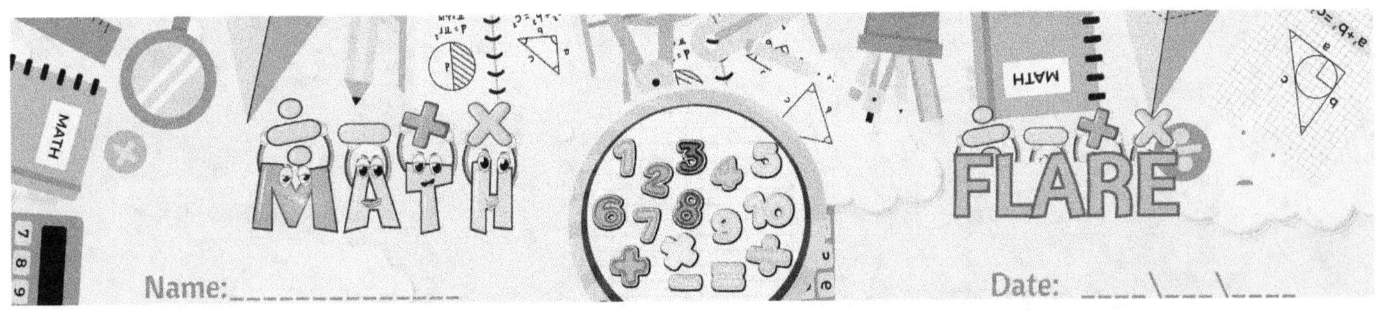

37.	38.	39.	40.
24 + 51	34 + 56	68 + 24	89 + 39

41.	42.	43.	44.
42 + 80	71 + 87	64 + 9	23 + 66

45.	46.	47.	48.
54 + 61	88 + 32	20 + 72	10 + 80

49.	50.	51.	52.
75 + 82	43 + 81	91 + 60	42 + 60

53.	54.	55.	56.
48 + 79	5 + 96	46 + 65	23 + 24

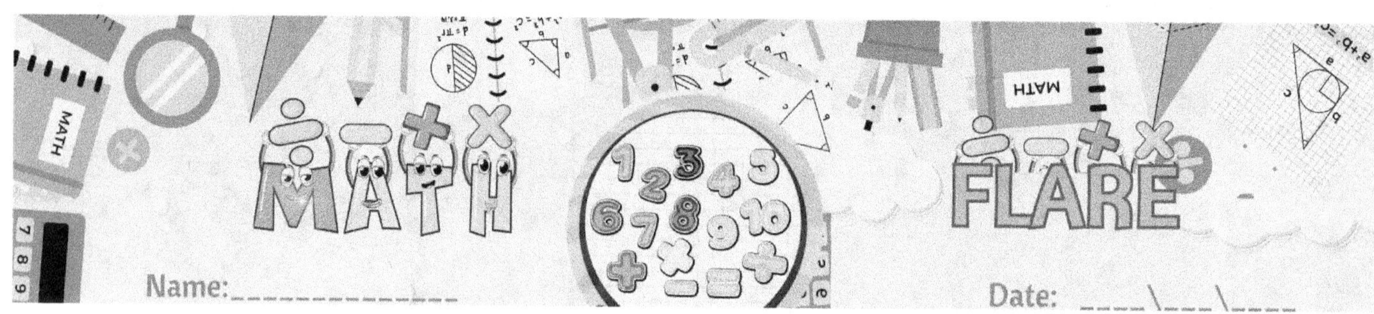

57. $\begin{array}{r} 92 \\ + 76 \\ \hline \end{array}$	58. $\begin{array}{r} 6 \\ + 33 \\ \hline \end{array}$	59. $\begin{array}{r} 26 \\ + 69 \\ \hline \end{array}$	60. $\begin{array}{r} 51 \\ + 27 \\ \hline \end{array}$
61. $\begin{array}{r} 63 \\ + 75 \\ \hline \end{array}$	62. $\begin{array}{r} 55 \\ + 70 \\ \hline \end{array}$	63. $\begin{array}{r} 91 \\ + 85 \\ \hline \end{array}$	64. $\begin{array}{r} 82 \\ + 52 \\ \hline \end{array}$
65. $\begin{array}{r} 42 \\ + 54 \\ \hline \end{array}$	66. $\begin{array}{r} 82 \\ + 85 \\ \hline \end{array}$	67. $\begin{array}{r} 80 \\ + 9 \\ \hline \end{array}$	68. $\begin{array}{r} 48 \\ + 81 \\ \hline \end{array}$
69. $\begin{array}{r} 39 \\ + 12 \\ \hline \end{array}$	70. $\begin{array}{r} 40 \\ + 85 \\ \hline \end{array}$	71. $\begin{array}{r} 6 \\ + 26 \\ \hline \end{array}$	72. $\begin{array}{r} 21 \\ + 89 \\ \hline \end{array}$
73. $\begin{array}{r} 39 \\ + 65 \\ \hline \end{array}$	74. $\begin{array}{r} 40 \\ + 45 \\ \hline \end{array}$	75. $\begin{array}{r} 67 \\ + 76 \\ \hline \end{array}$	76. $\begin{array}{r} 55 \\ + 7 \\ \hline \end{array}$

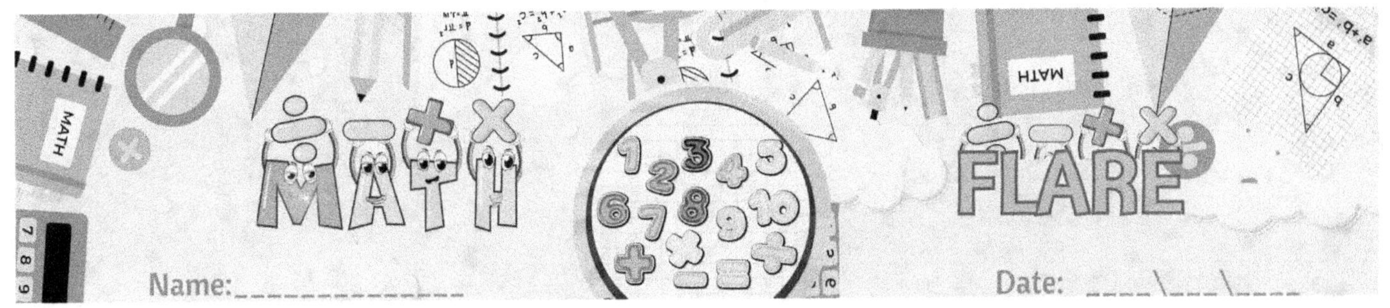

Name:________________   Date:_______________

77. 32 + 17	78. 19 + 16	79. 6 + 72	80. 69 + 63
81. 97 + 53	82. 55 + 91	83. 83 + 37	84. 44 + 84
85. 28 + 25	86. 94 + 15	87. 29 + 66	88. 23 + 38
89. 55 + 66	90. 31 + 27	91. 46 + 38	92. 85 + 66
93. 100 + 76	94. 54 + 64	95. 91 + 33	96. 76 + 67

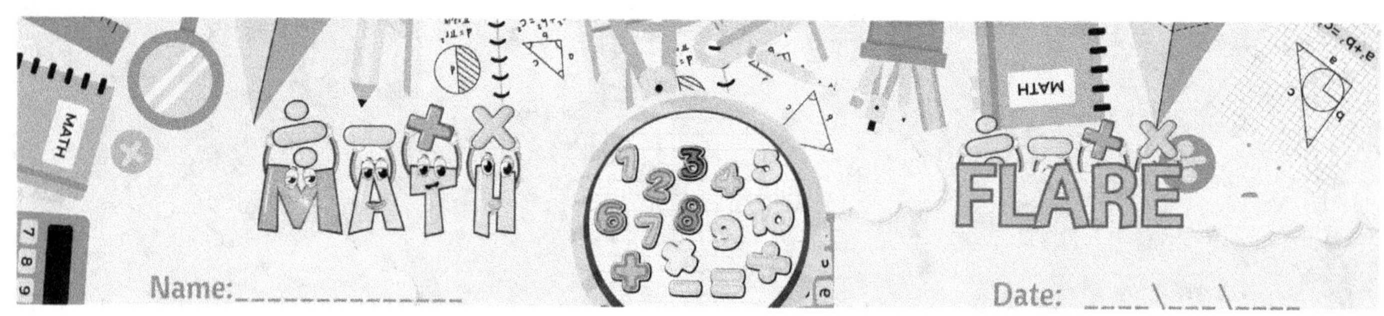

97. 43 + 78	98. 88 + 53	99. 71 + 30	100. 7 + 3
101. 22 + 56	102. 17 + 43	103. 82 + 41	104. 78 + 67
105. 94 + 81	106. 62 + 41	107. 42 + 42	108. 18 + 60
109. 68 + 90	110. 92 + 9	111. 83 + 79	112. 93 + 96
113. 50 + 28	114. 72 + 51	115. 78 + 70	116. 67 + 26

Subtraction: 1 through 100

Find the Difference.

117. 64 − 19	118. 15 − 14	119. 29 − 13	120. 85 − 51
121. 98 − 86	122. 73 − 8	123. 74 − 27	124. 33 − 1
125. 65 − 19	126. 87 − 70	127. 43 − 42	128. 27 − 12
129. 66 − 14	130. 94 − 51	131. 72 − 20	132. 90 − 23

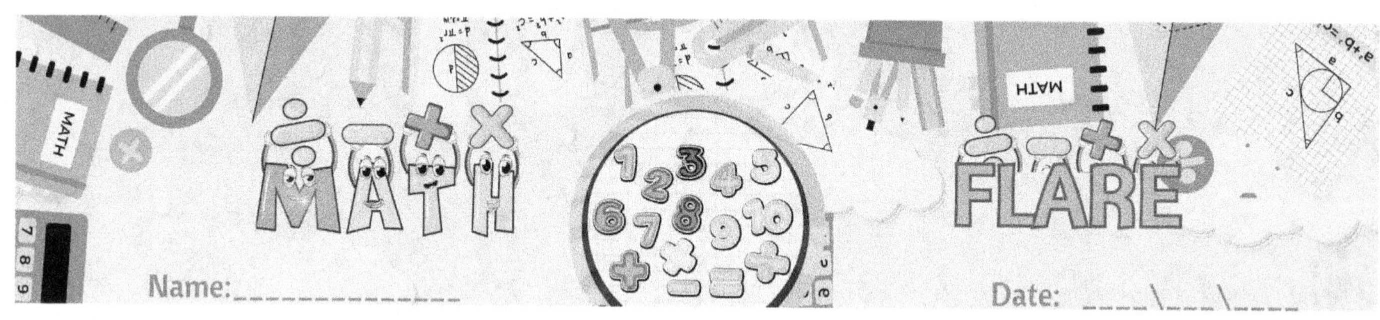

133.	134.	135.	136.
23 - 9	82 - 11	42 - 12	45 - 12

137.	138.	139.	140.
15 - 6	19 - 18	18 - 15	32 - 5

141.	142.	143.	144.
12 - 9	91 - 45	86 - 74	89 - 56

145.	146.	147.	148.
18 - 12	35 - 1	55 - 17	92 - 66

149.	150.	151.	152.
99 - 45	96 - 34	60 - 8	68 - 24

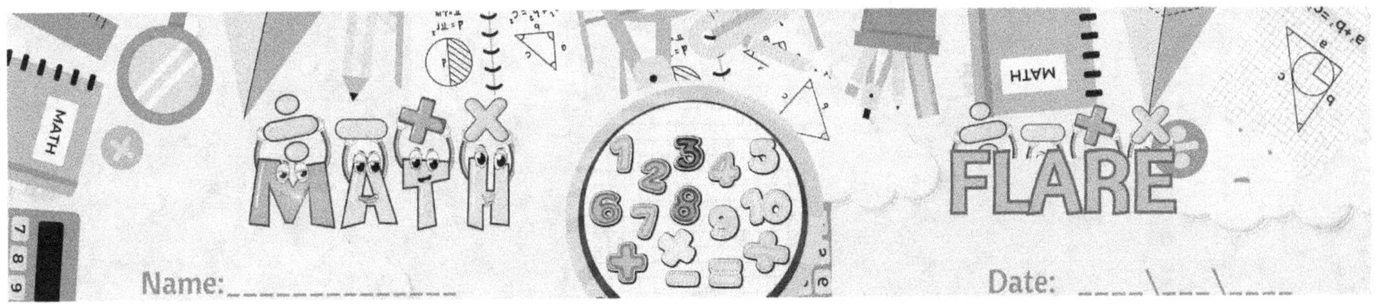

153.   91
    − 56
	154. 77
	    − 5
		155. 89
		    − 22
			156. 39
			    − 31

157.   96
    − 77
	158. 57
	    − 56
		159. 43
		    − 17
			160. 46
			    − 14

161.   53
    − 10
	162. 13
	    − 10
		163. 99
		    − 38
			164. 77
			    − 59

165.   47
    − 19
	166. 97
	    − 62
		167. 89
		    − 80
			168. 62
			    − 55

169.   15
    − 9
	170. 64
	    − 16
		171. 20
		    − 17
			172. 77
			    − 66

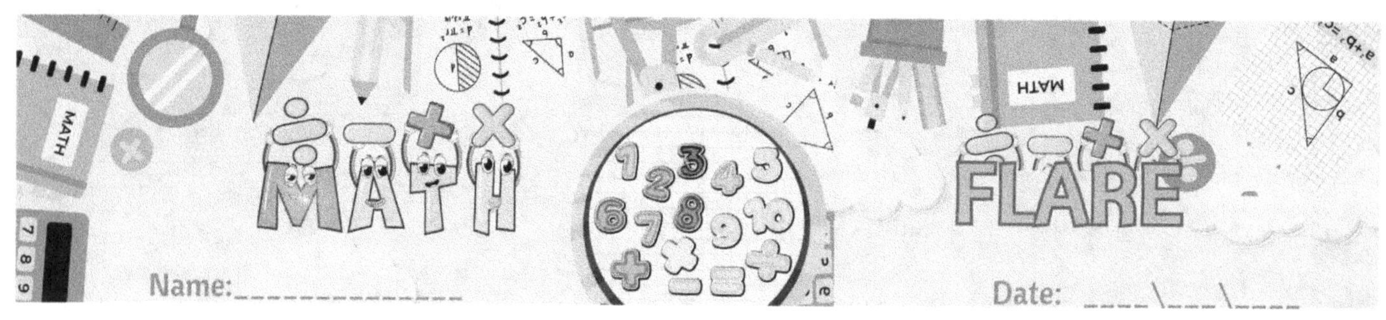

173. $\begin{array}{r} 39 \\ -\ 20 \\ \hline \end{array}$	174. $\begin{array}{r} 14 \\ -\ 10 \\ \hline \end{array}$	175. $\begin{array}{r} 79 \\ -\ 74 \\ \hline \end{array}$	176. $\begin{array}{r} 41 \\ -\ 25 \\ \hline \end{array}$
177. $\begin{array}{r} 15 \\ -\ 10 \\ \hline \end{array}$	178. $\begin{array}{r} 89 \\ -\ 34 \\ \hline \end{array}$	179. $\begin{array}{r} 18 \\ -\ 17 \\ \hline \end{array}$	180. $\begin{array}{r} 41 \\ -\ 22 \\ \hline \end{array}$
181. $\begin{array}{r} 87 \\ -\ 85 \\ \hline \end{array}$	182. $\begin{array}{r} 67 \\ -\ 33 \\ \hline \end{array}$	183. $\begin{array}{r} 34 \\ -\ 24 \\ \hline \end{array}$	184. $\begin{array}{r} 92 \\ -\ 7 \\ \hline \end{array}$
185. $\begin{array}{r} 29 \\ -\ 19 \\ \hline \end{array}$	186. $\begin{array}{r} 93 \\ -\ 75 \\ \hline \end{array}$	187. $\begin{array}{r} 82 \\ -\ 14 \\ \hline \end{array}$	188. $\begin{array}{r} 25 \\ -\ 16 \\ \hline \end{array}$
189. $\begin{array}{r} 49 \\ -\ 10 \\ \hline \end{array}$	190. $\begin{array}{r} 46 \\ -\ 24 \\ \hline \end{array}$	191. $\begin{array}{r} 40 \\ -\ 3 \\ \hline \end{array}$	192. $\begin{array}{r} 100 \\ -\ 49 \\ \hline \end{array}$

Name:________________   Date: _______________

193. 63 – 13	194. 12 – 3	195. 29 – 3	196. 44 – 7
197. 28 – 8	198. 62 – 40	199. 62 – 61	200. 54 – 8
201. 10 – 6	202. 82 – 73	203. 56 – 14	204. 94 – 85
205. 58 – 49	206. 27 – 22	207. 99 – 16	208. 49 – 44
209. 19 – 14	210. 14 – 14	211. 84 – 68	212. 63 – 46

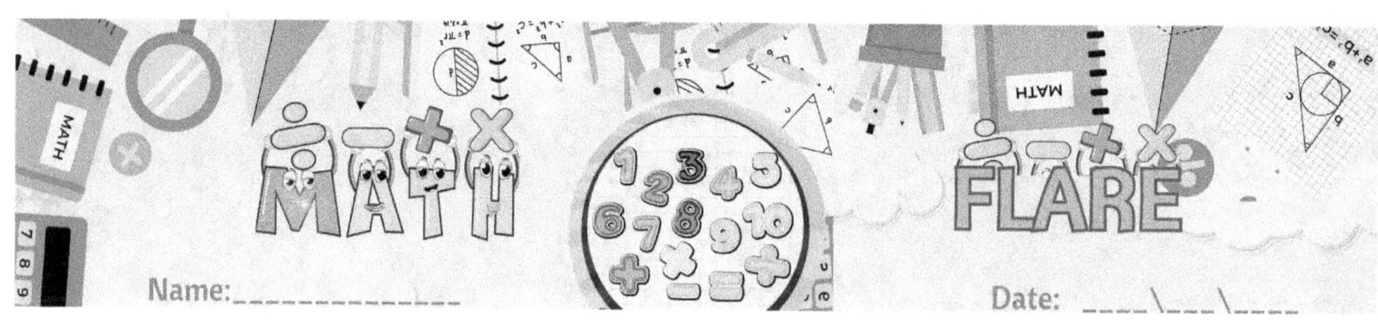

213. 81 − 4	214. 50 − 10	215. 64 − 49	216. 93 − 32
217. 60 − 52	218. 53 − 28	219. 62 − 44	220. 72 − 57
221. 35 − 32	222. 63 − 24	223. 89 − 51	224. 23 − 2
225. 85 − 59	226. 59 − 51	227. 95 − 47	228. 38 − 9
229. 95 − 8	230. 19 − 9	231. 80 − 61	232. 37 − 29

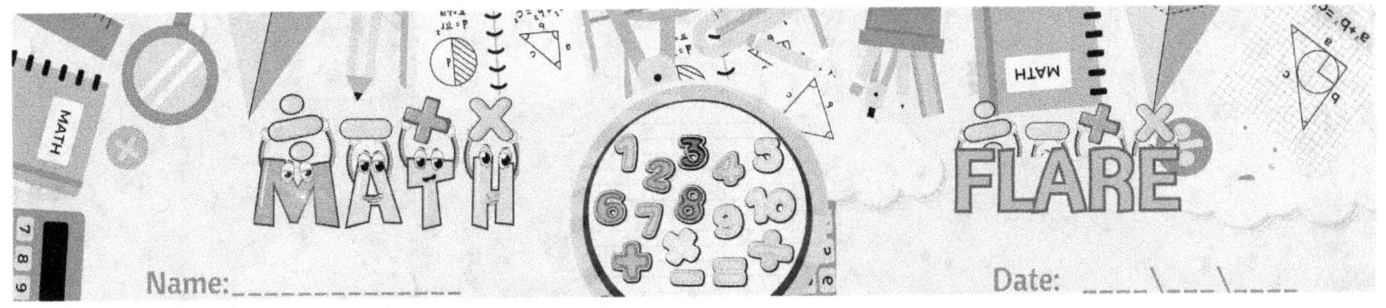

Addition with Regrouping

Find the sum.

233. 92 + 88	234. 26 + 99	235. 68 + 92	236. 33 + 78
237. 3 + 28	238. 72 + 99	239. 22 + 89	240. 84 + 29
241. 89 + 42	242. 35 + 98	243. 23 + 7	244. 41 + 9
245. 55 + 78	246. 57 + 56	247. 61 + 49	248. 2 + 59
249. 61 + 89	250. 46 + 4	251. 33 + 7	252. 37 + 95

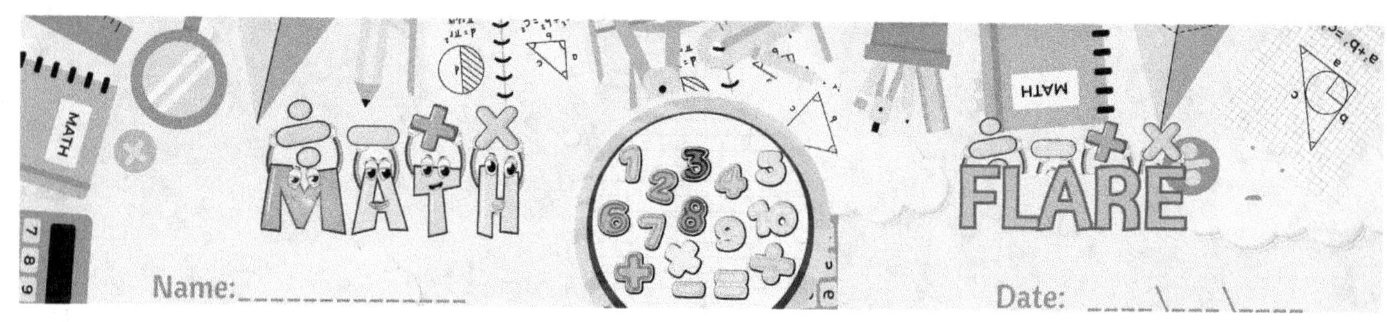

253. 85 + 75	254. 77 + 39	255. 99 + 73	256. 25 + 89
257. 59 + 78	258. 41 + 89	259. 55 + 86	260. 46 + 89
261. 58 + 89	262. 36 + 87	263. 81 + 89	264. 24 + 87
265. 33 + 77	266. 77 + 87	267. 89 + 87	268. 6 + 44
269. 56 + 9	270. 22 + 98	271. 31 + 79	272. 29 + 83

273. $\begin{array}{r} 27 \\ +\ 98 \\ \hline \end{array}$	274. $\begin{array}{r} 64 \\ +\ 68 \\ \hline \end{array}$	275. $\begin{array}{r} 13 \\ +\ 98 \\ \hline \end{array}$	276. $\begin{array}{r} 28 \\ +\ 93 \\ \hline \end{array}$
277. $\begin{array}{r} 58 \\ +\ 85 \\ \hline \end{array}$	278. $\begin{array}{r} 45 \\ +\ 96 \\ \hline \end{array}$	279. $\begin{array}{r} 56 \\ +\ 54 \\ \hline \end{array}$	280. $\begin{array}{r} 34 \\ +\ 6 \\ \hline \end{array}$
281. $\begin{array}{r} 47 \\ +\ 98 \\ \hline \end{array}$	282. $\begin{array}{r} 7 \\ +\ 64 \\ \hline \end{array}$	283. $\begin{array}{r} 97 \\ +\ 44 \\ \hline \end{array}$	284. $\begin{array}{r} 1 \\ +\ 79 \\ \hline \end{array}$
285. $\begin{array}{r} 33 \\ +\ 98 \\ \hline \end{array}$	286. $\begin{array}{r} 83 \\ +\ 47 \\ \hline \end{array}$	287. $\begin{array}{r} 64 \\ +\ 77 \\ \hline \end{array}$	288. $\begin{array}{r} 88 \\ +\ 42 \\ \hline \end{array}$
289. $\begin{array}{r} 13 \\ +\ 99 \\ \hline \end{array}$	290. $\begin{array}{r} 58 \\ +\ 68 \\ \hline \end{array}$	291. $\begin{array}{r} 16 \\ +\ 95 \\ \hline \end{array}$	292. $\begin{array}{r} 8 \\ +\ 12 \\ \hline \end{array}$

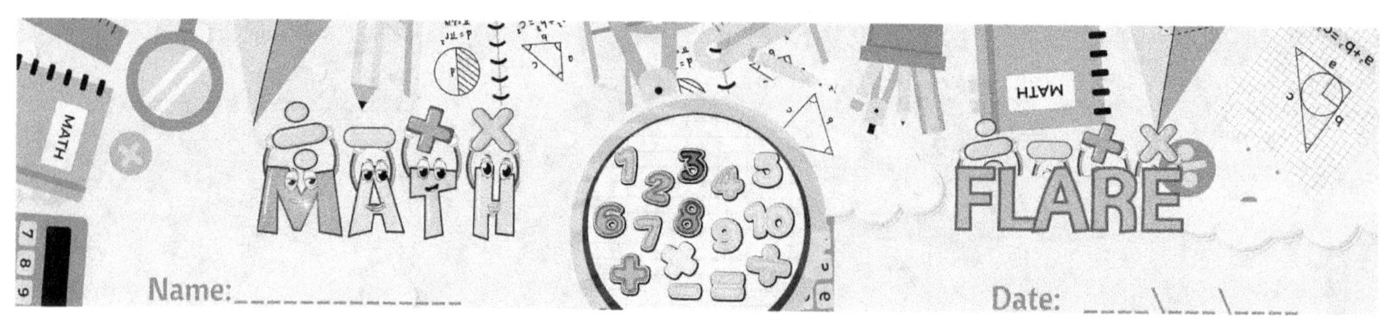

293. 12 + 99	294. 24 + 96	295. 43 + 87	296. 88 + 4
297. 75 + 38	298. 24 + 99	299. 11 + 99	300. 87 + 83
301. 71 + 99	302. 32 + 89	303. 39 + 81	304. 96 + 88
305. 27 + 3	306. 84 + 9	307. 96 + 24	308. 51 + 99
309. 49 + 89	310. 21 + 99	311. 29 + 84	312. 73 + 48

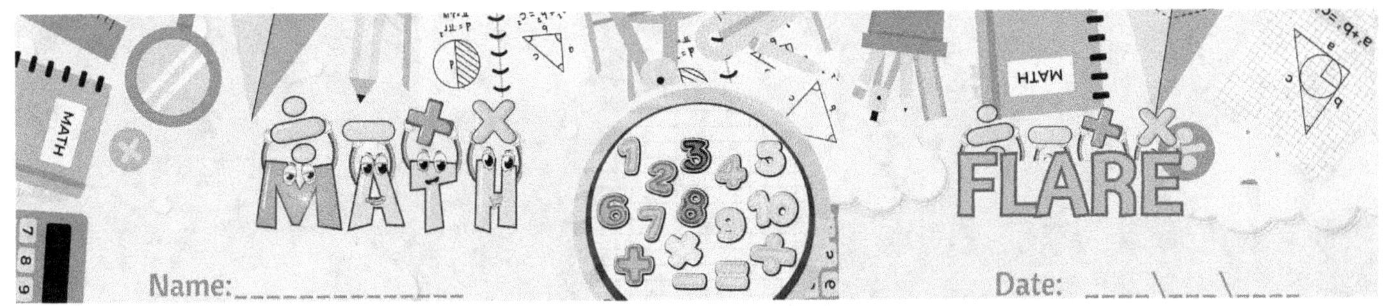

313. 54 + 96	314. 32 + 78	315. 66 + 75	316. 41 + 99
317. 29 + 93	318. 73 + 37	319. 21 + 89	320. 49 + 91
321. 27 + 84	322. 8 + 57	323. 28 + 97	324. 23 + 87
325. 21 + 9	326. 63 + 47	327. 64 + 87	328. 5 + 59
329. 9 + 58	330. 28 + 92	331. 72 + 49	332. 39 + 72

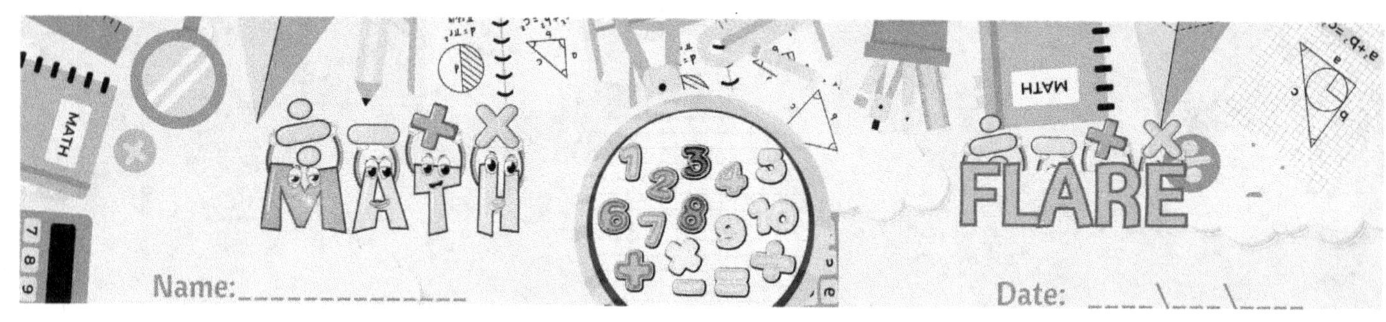

333. 83 + 67	334. 59 + 57	335. 23 + 99	336. 61 + 79
337. 78 + 89	338. 97 + 27	339. 74 + 99	340. 93 + 19
341. 26 + 89	342. 89 + 65	343. 24 + 89	344. 16 + 97
345. 69 + 87	346. 46 + 85	347. 68 + 67	348. 77 + 66
349. 94 + 9	350. 47 + 85	351. 67 + 76	352. 12 + 98

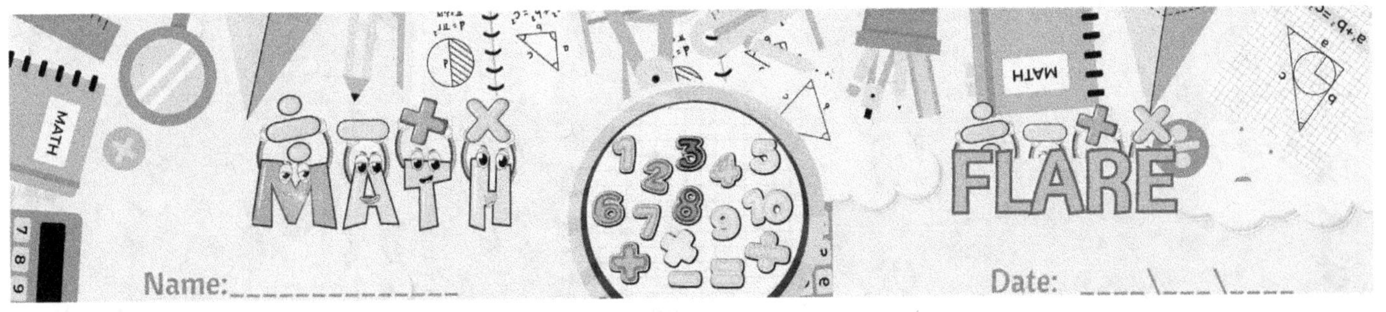

Subtraction with Regrouping

Find the difference.

353.
$$80 - 69$$

354.
$$30 - 4$$

355.
$$20 - 12$$

356.
$$10 - 2$$

357.
$$80 - 7$$

358.
$$40 - 27$$

359.
$$9 - 6$$

360.
$$40 - 9$$

361.
$$10 - 6$$

362.
$$50 - 21$$

363.
$$20 - 5$$

364.
$$20 - 3$$

365.
$$20 - 7$$

366.
$$10 - 4$$

367.
$$30 - 13$$

368.
$$6 - 2$$

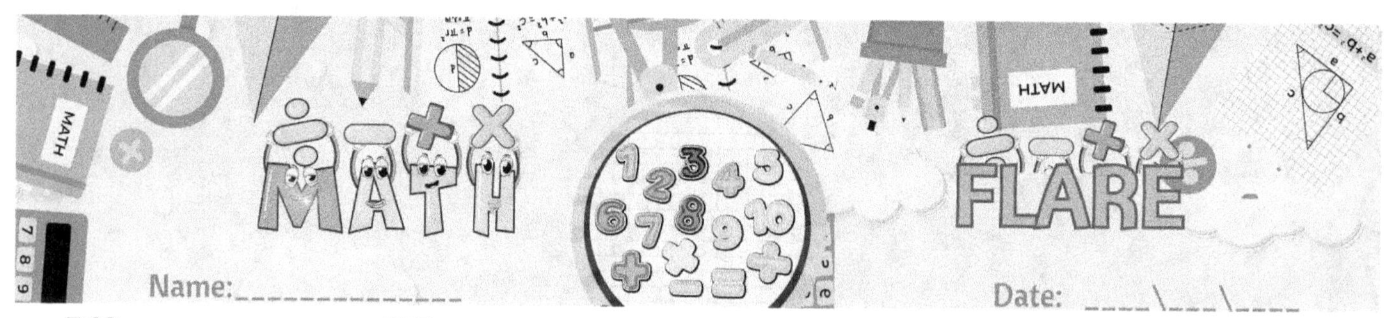

Name:____________   Date: ____________

369.   10
       − 7
       ______

370.   70
       − 57
       ______

371.   50
       − 19
       ______

372.   90
       − 77
       ______

373.   7
       − 4
       ______

374.   20
       − 6
       ______

375.   50
       − 2
       ______

376.   90
       − 87
       ______

377.   30
       − 22
       ______

378.   60
       − 55
       ______

379.   30
       − 27
       ______

380.   60
       − 53
       ______

381.   50
       − 13
       ______

382.   30
       − 17
       ______

383.   70
       − 42
       ______

384.   40
       − 24
       ______

385.   20
       − 2
       ______

386.   30
       − 6
       ______

387.   10
       − 1
       ______

388.   4
       − 3
       ______

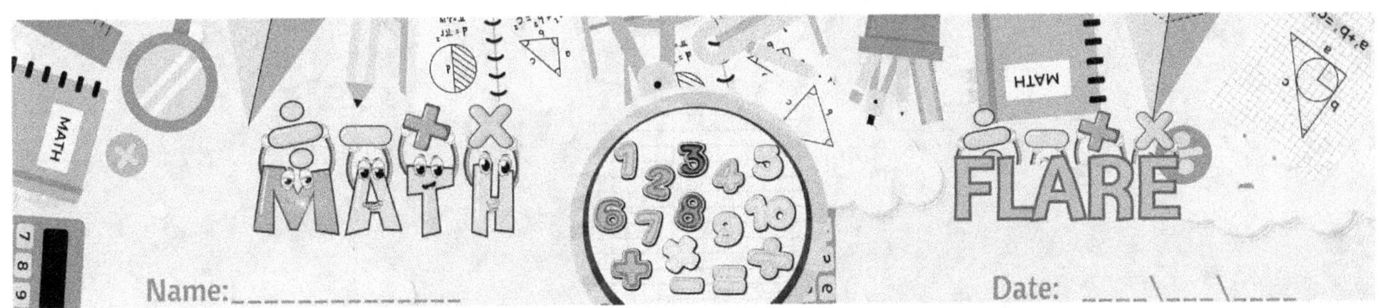

389. 6 − 1	390. 80 − 74	391. 8 − 4	392. 4 − 4
393. 60 − 48	394. 60 − 38	395. 90 − 64	396. 90 − 23
397. 40 − 19	398. 50 − 39	399. 50 − 15	400. 20 − 11
401. 70 − 61	402. 40 − 17	403. 1 − 1	404. 40 − 2
405. 70 − 45	406. 80 − 12	407. 60 − 26	408. 80 − 3

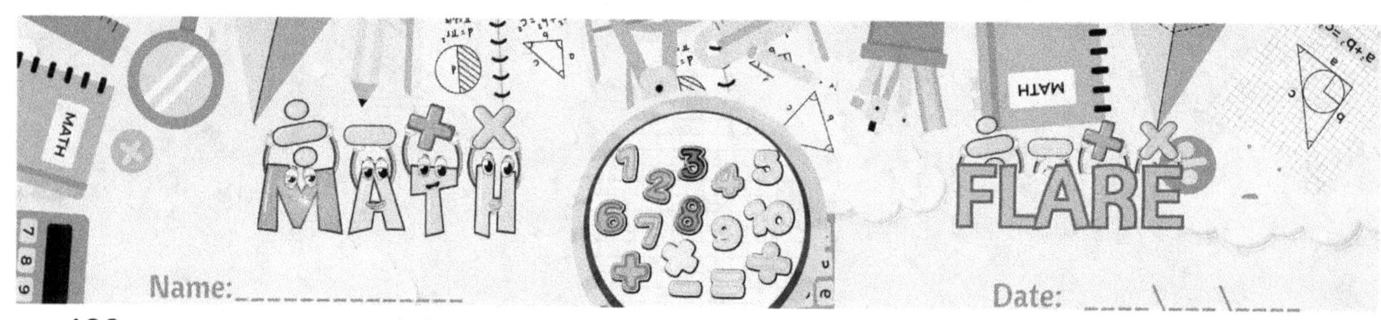

409.	60 − 8	410.	90 − 63	411.	70 − 49	412.	100 − 72
413.	20 − 17	414.	5 − 2	415.	70 − 37	416.	30 − 15
417.	30 − 11	418.	70 − 8	419.	90 − 86	420.	50 − 16
421.	30 − 5	422.	2 − 1	423.	70 − 11	424.	20 − 13
425.	90 − 55	426.	80 − 49	427.	90 − 65	428.	70 − 52

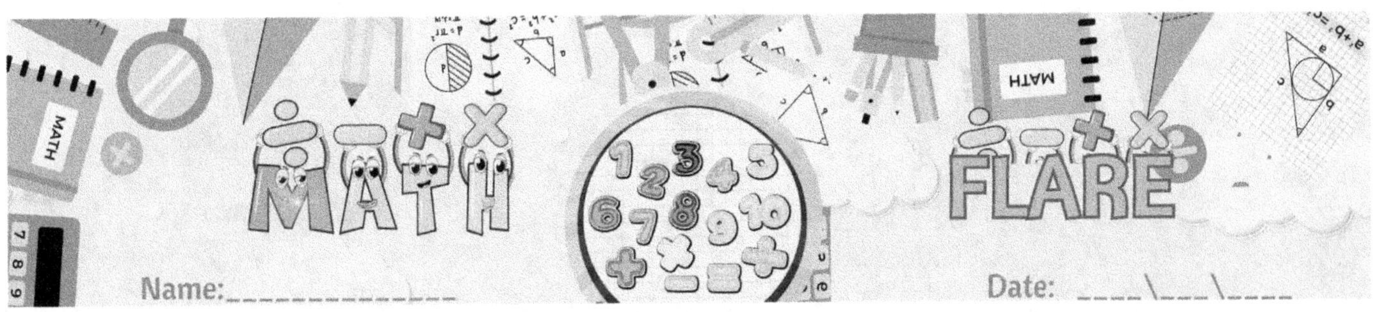

429. 30 − 14	430. 50 − 45	431. 60 − 32	432. 50 − 23
433. 30 − 8	434. 60 − 21	435. 90 − 45	436. 9 − 3
437. 80 − 45	438. 40 − 12	439. 100 − 67	440. 40 − 5
441. 90 − 49	442. 60 − 28	443. 30 − 9	444. 60 − 9
445. 30 − 2	446. 90 − 28	447. 30 − 25	448. 90 − 75

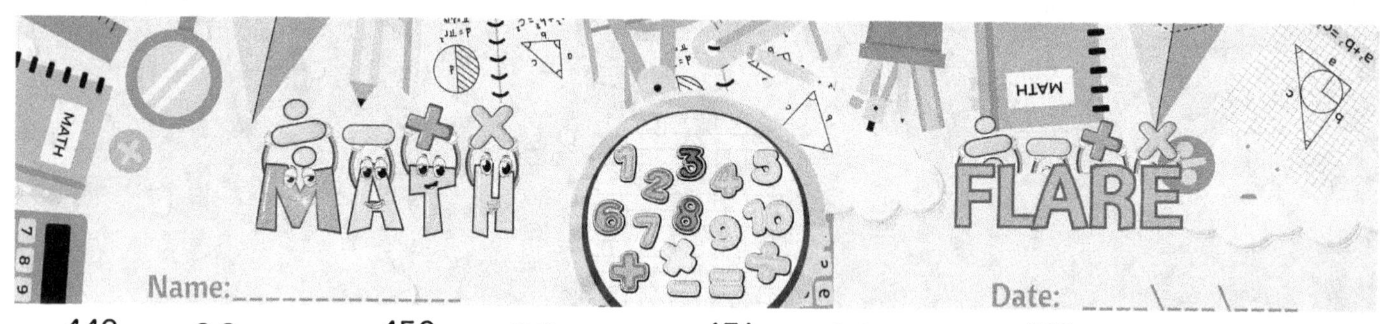

449. 80 − 65	450. 90 − 5	451. 90 − 9	452. 80 − 57
453. 40 − 3	454. 50 − 43	455. 60 − 11	456. 7 − 3
457. 70 − 6	458. 10 − 5	459. 30 − 18	460. 80 − 24
461. 60 − 24	462. 40 − 34	463. 40 − 16	464. 90 − 53
465. 80 − 22	466. 20 − 8	467. 3 − 1	468. 90 − 59

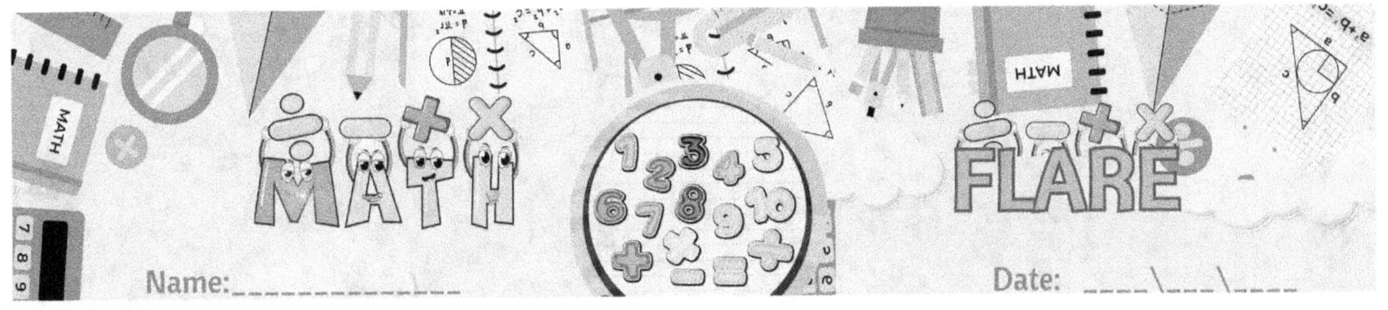

Make 100

Add a number to the first number to make 100.

469. $30 + \underline{\quad} = 100$

470. $11 + \underline{\quad} = 100$

471. $51 + \underline{\quad} = 100$

472. $46 + \underline{\quad} = 100$

473. $24 + \underline{\quad} = 100$

474. $42 + \underline{\quad} = 100$

475. $69 + \underline{\quad} = 100$

476. $41 + \underline{\quad} = 100$

477. $95 + \underline{\quad} = 100$

478. $20 + \underline{\quad} = 100$

479. $70 + \underline{\quad} = 100$

480. $45 + \underline{\quad} = 100$

481. $28 + \underline{\quad} = 100$

482. $19 + \underline{\quad} = 100$

483. $2 + \underline{\quad} = 100$

484. $21 + \underline{\quad} = 100$

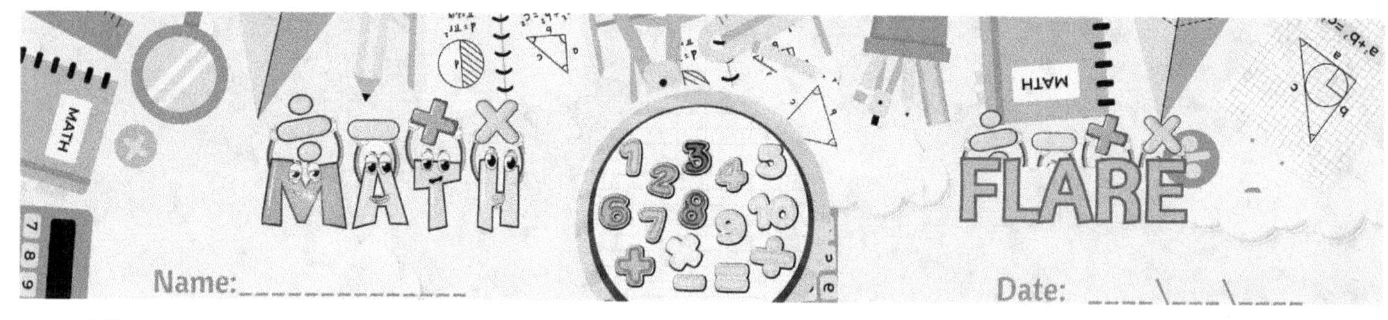

485. 10 + ___ = 100

486. 4 + ___ = 100

487. 93 + ___ = 100

488. 16 + ___ = 100

489. 97 + ___ = 100

490. 44 + ___ = 100

491. 77 + ___ = 100

492. 7 + ___ = 100

493. 62 + ___ = 100

494. 63 + ___ = 100

495. 64 + ___ = 100

496. 60 + ___ = 100

497. 55 + ___ = 100

498. 57 + ___ = 100

499. 79 + ___ = 100

500. 49 + ___ = 100

501. 9 + ___ = 100

502. 96 + ___ = 100

503. 22 + ___ = 100

504. 67 + ___ = 100

505. 48 + ___ = 100

506. 61 + ___ = 100

507. 80 + ___ = 100

508. 100 + ___ = 100

509. 73 + ___ = 100

510. 83 + ___ = 100

511. 35 + ___ = 100

512. 6 + ___ = 100

513. 25 + ___ = 100

514. 29 + ___ = 100

515. 13 + ___ = 100

516. 98 + ___ = 100

517. 85 + ___ = 100

518. 27 + ___ = 100

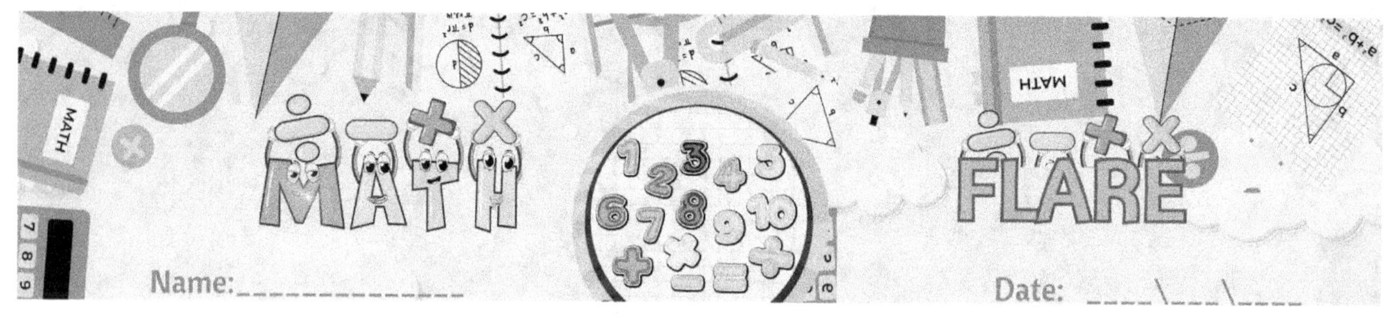

Addition: Unknown Number

Find the unknown number.

519. 2 + ____ = 26

520. ____ + 4 = 27

521. 86 + ____ = 173

522. 71 + 96 = ____

523. 24 + 46 = ____

524. 32 + 79 = ____

525. ____ + 3 = 102

526. ____ + 25 = 85

527. 3 + 15 = ____

528. 10 + 74 = ____

529. ____ + 92 = 116

530. 44 + 61 = ____

531. 24 + ____ = 83

532. ____ + 2 = 32

533. ____ + 25 = 45

534. ____ + 31 = 51

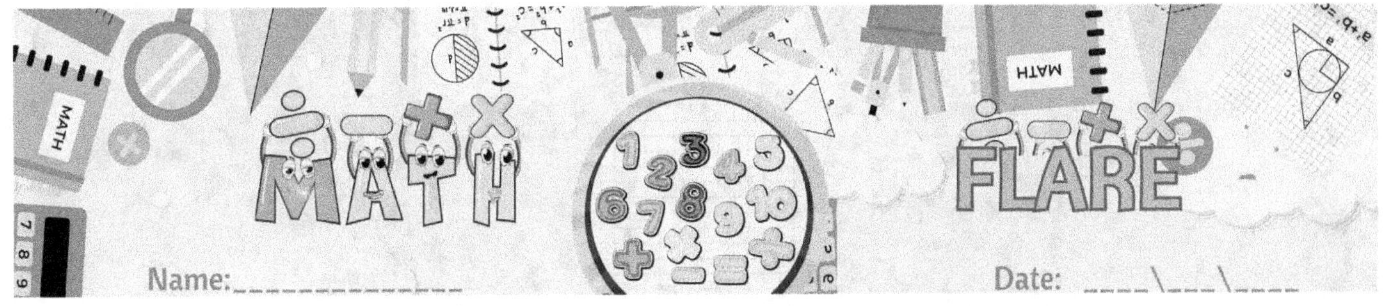

Name:______________ Date: _______________

535. 47 + ____ = 83

536. 93 + 97 = ____

537. 73 + 39 = ____

538. 81 + 4 = ____

539. 54 + 54 = ____

540. 6 + ____ = 38

541. ____ + 18 = 31

542. 14 + 51 = ____

543. 39 + 65 = ____

544. 18 + ____ = 20

545. 76 + ____ = 160

546. 5 + ____ = 15

547. 80 + 62 = ____

548. 80 + ____ = 108

549. 58 + ____ = 128

550. ____ + 99 = 176

551. ____ + 2 = 29

552. 33 + ____ = 96

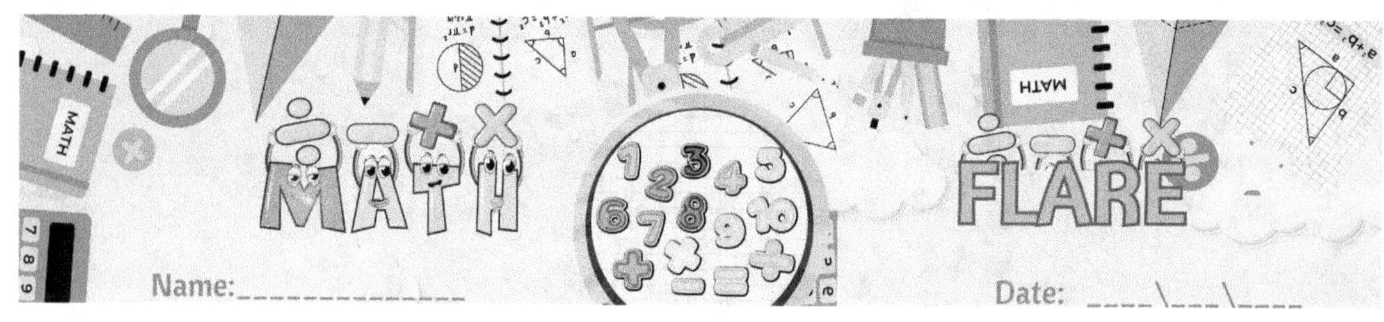

553. _____ + 64 = 74

554. _____ + 63 = 116

555. 33 + 7 = _____

556. 21 + 69 = _____

557. 87 + _____ = 100

558. _____ + 6 = 55

559. 46 + _____ = 125

560. 64 + 55 = _____

561. 9 + _____ = 28

562. 56 + _____ = 119

563. 33 + 84 = _____

564. 17 + _____ = 29

565. 59 + _____ = 114

566. 47 + _____ = 132

567. _____ + 7 = 84

568. 6 + 12 = _____

569. 85 + 51 = _____

570. 42 + 75 = _____

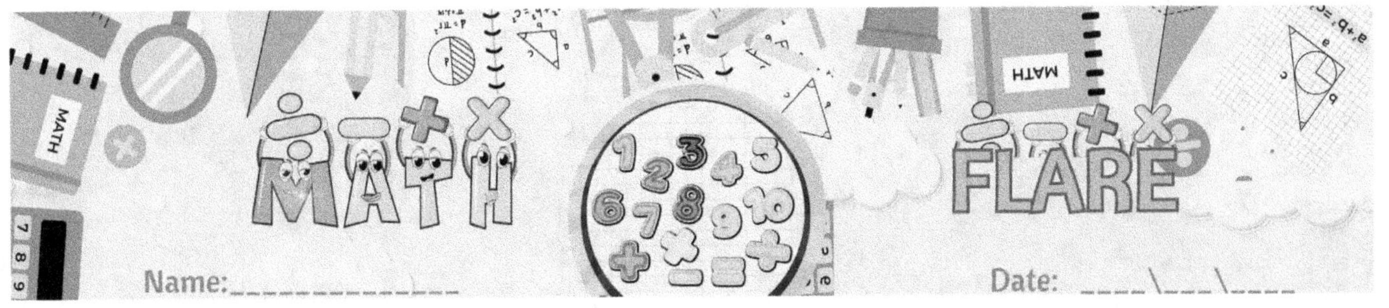

571. 13 + 54 = _____

572. _____ + 70 = 139

573. 64 + _____ = 99

574. _____ + 68 = 90

575. _____ + 75 = 89

576. 82 + 79 = _____

577. _____ + 23 = 30

578. _____ + 8 = 99

579. 47 + _____ = 117

580. 32 + _____ = 58

581. _____ + 42 = 89

582. 5 + _____ = 84

583. _____ + 37 = 97

584. _____ + 82 = 174

585. 8 + _____ = 45

586. 21 + 95 = _____

587. 38 + 89 = _____

588. 43 + 54 = _____

589. $50 + \underline{\hspace{1cm}} = 136$

590. $98 + \underline{\hspace{1cm}} = 195$

591. $63 + \underline{\hspace{1cm}} = 112$

592. $98 + \underline{\hspace{1cm}} = 182$

593. $72 + \underline{\hspace{1cm}} = 140$

594. $\underline{\hspace{1cm}} + 55 = 134$

595. $\underline{\hspace{1cm}} + 98 = 114$

596. $66 + 17 = \underline{\hspace{1cm}}$

597. $\underline{\hspace{1cm}} + 17 = 37$

598. $\underline{\hspace{1cm}} + 72 = 101$

599. $50 + 90 = \underline{\hspace{1cm}}$

600. $11 + 29 = \underline{\hspace{1cm}}$

601. $43 + \underline{\hspace{1cm}} = 84$

602. $\underline{\hspace{1cm}} + 77 = 139$

603. $55 + \underline{\hspace{1cm}} = 142$

604. $42 + 18 = \underline{\hspace{1cm}}$

605. $\underline{\hspace{1cm}} + 38 = 118$

606. $59 + 61 = \underline{\hspace{1cm}}$

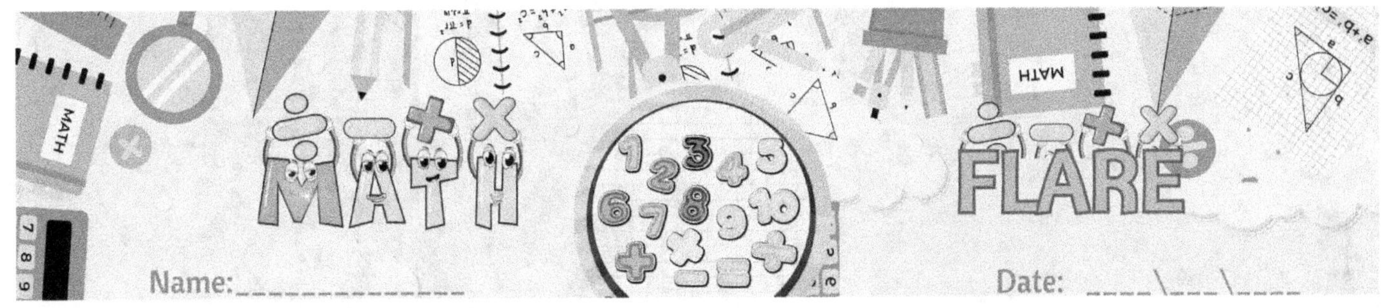

607. _____ + 34 = 105

608. _____ + 98 = 162

609. _____ + 21 = 64

610. _____ + 92 = 99

611. 58 + 38 = _____

612. _____ + 10 = 77

613. 72 + 5 = _____

614. 75 + 22 = _____

615. 61 + _____ = 132

616. _____ + 60 = 65

617. _____ + 71 = 147

618. 55 + 23 = _____

619. _____ + 22 = 109

620. 30 + _____ = 115

621. 27 + _____ = 89

622. _____ + 77 = 152

623. _____ + 6 = 46

624. 45 + _____ = 131

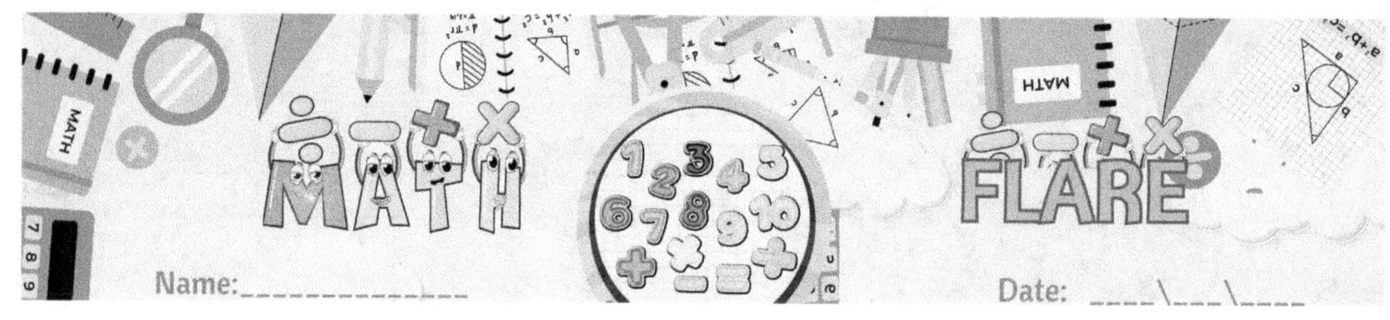

625. _____ + 31 = 84

626. 29 + _____ = 58

627. 84 + 18 = _____

628. _____ + 6 = 77

629. 74 + 53 = _____

630. _____ + 51 = 57

631. 13 + 21 = _____

632. 57 + 10 = _____

633. _____ + 99 = 133

634. 85 + _____ = 87

635. _____ + 42 = 121

636. 12 + 22 = _____

637. 91 + 22 = _____

638. 67 + _____ = 163

639. 63 + 90 = _____

640. 70 + _____ = 137

641. 60 + 90 = _____

642. 69 + 32 = _____

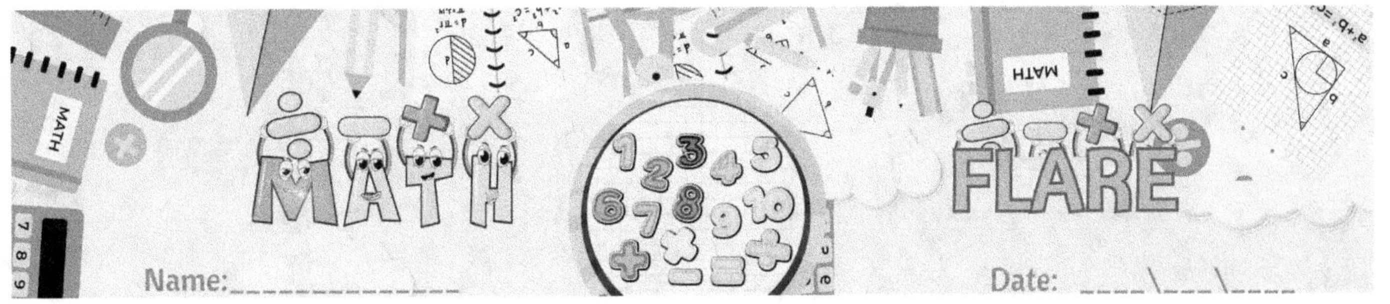

643. 43 + 76 = _____

644. _____ + 58 = 133

645. 100 + _____ = 150

646. _____ + 36 = 85

647. 18 + 80 = _____

648. 73 + _____ = 79

649. 6 + 66 = _____

650. _____ + 41 = 86

651. 20 + _____ = 65

652. _____ + 12 = 20

653. _____ + 8 = 28

654. 38 + _____ = 101

655. _____ + 75 = 127

656. 43 + _____ = 127

657. 83 + 39 = _____

658. _____ + 23 = 113

659. 53 + _____ = 79

660. 67 + 58 = _____

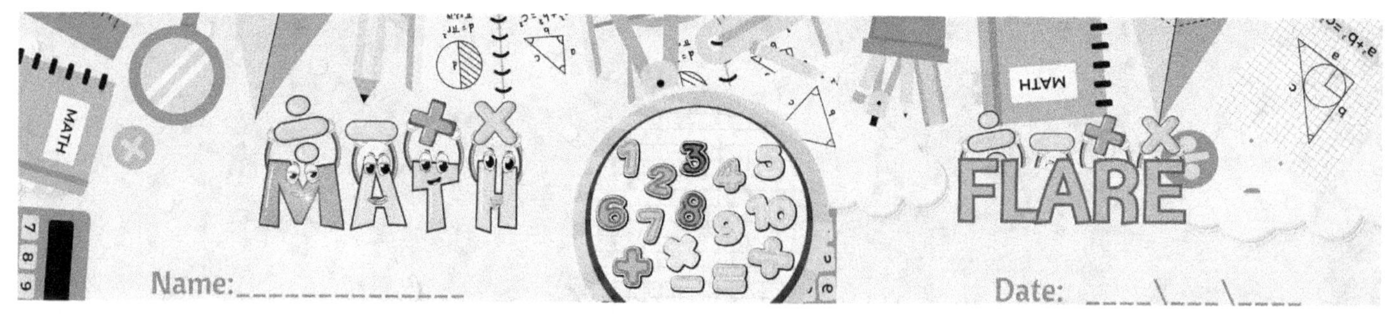

Subtraction: Unknown Number

Find the unknown number.

661. ____ - 9 = 22

662. 11 - 4 = ____

663. ____ - 71 = 22

664. 14 - 3 = ____

665. ____ - 33 = 21

666. 91 - 88 = ____

667. 51 - 15 = ____

668. 52 - ____ = 43

669. 84 - 48 = ____

670. 20 - ____ = 12

671. ____ - 6 = 38

672. 16 - 5 = ____

673. 17 - 11 = ____

674. 57 - ____ = 12

675. 90 - 46 = ____

676. 58 - 47 = ____

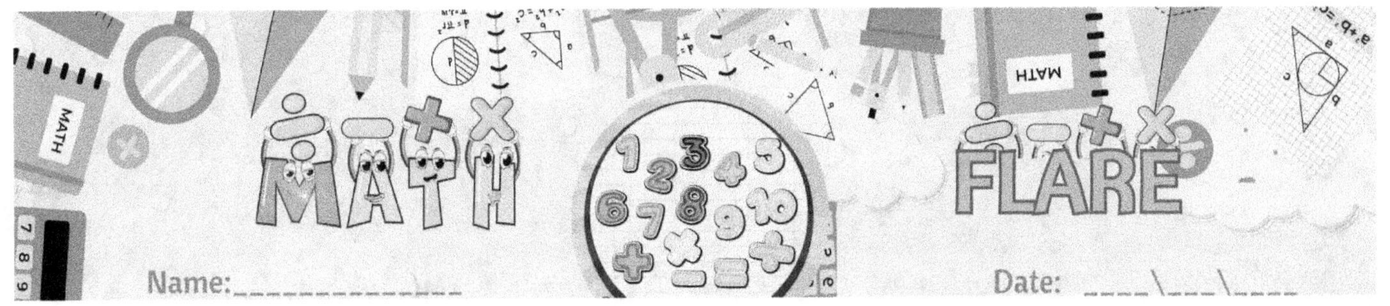

677. 99 - ____ = 13

678. ____ - 23 = 2

679. 49 - 38 = ____

680. ____ - 12 = 15

681. 13 - 4 = ____

682. ____ - 20 = 2

683. 87 - ____ = 47

684. 45 - 25 = ____

685. 92 - 69 = ____

686. 46 - ____ = 2

687. 22 - 8 = ____

688. 28 - 4 = ____

689. ____ - 22 = 6

690. 29 - ____ = 20

691. ____ - 30 = 0

692. 17 - ____ = 14

693. ____ - 58 = 40

694. ____ - 12 = 9

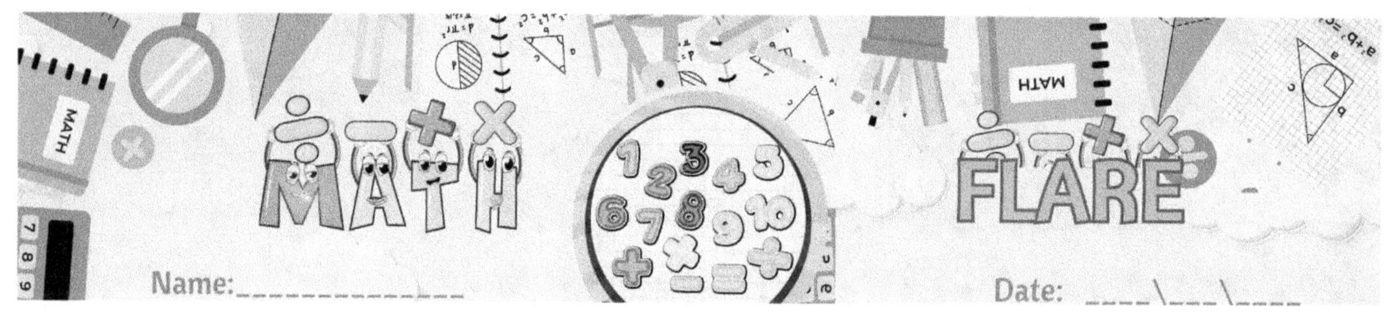

695. 76 - ____ = 72

696. 44 - 30 = ____

697. 39 - 6 = ____

698. 99 - 18 = ____

699. 45 - 28 = ____

700. 33 - ____ = 1

701. 89 - ____ = 75

702. ____ - 11 = 8

703. 70 - 48 = ____

704. ____ - 5 = 66

705. 75 - 50 = ____

706. 61 - ____ = 5

707. 13 - ____ = 10

708. 83 - ____ = 20

709. 52 - 42 = ____

710. 48 - ____ = 30

711. ____ - 5 = 6

712. 62 - 29 = ____

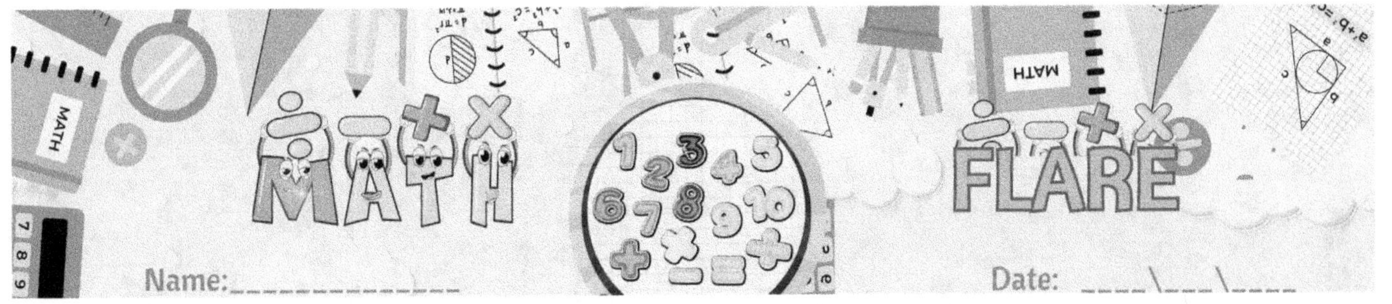

713. 100 - _____ = 92

714. _____ - 2 = 19

715. 43 - 26 = _____

716. 12 - 4 = _____

717. 44 - _____ = 40

718. 49 - _____ = 33

719. 92 - 7 = _____

720. 85 - 6 = _____

721. _____ - 25 = 28

722. 53 - 29 = _____

723. _____ - 15 = 3

724. _____ - 27 = 15

725. 24 - _____ = 13

726. 60 - 31 = _____

727. 22 - _____ = 5

728. 100 - _____ = 78

729. 71 - 43 = _____

730. 94 - 64 = _____

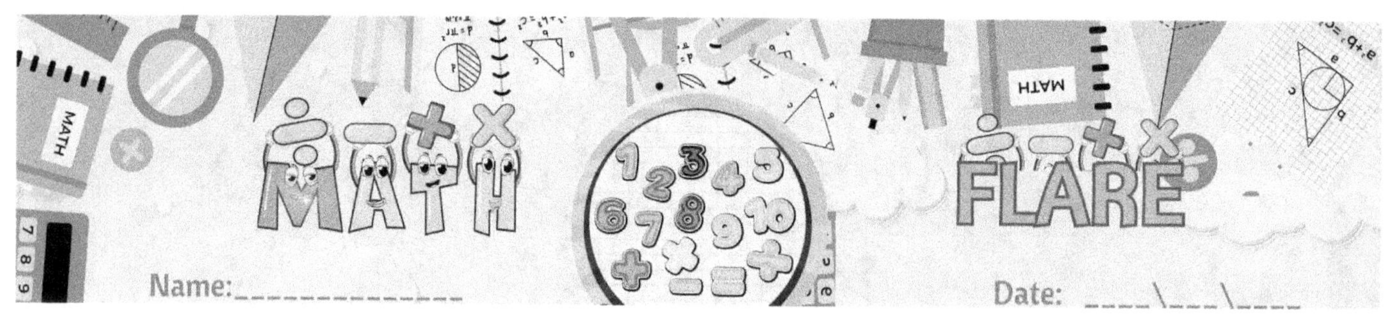

731. _____ - 36 = 1

732. 90 - _____ = 5

733. _____ - 43 = 2

734. _____ - 11 = 23

735. 39 - 7 = _____

736. 90 - _____ = 57

737. _____ - 55 = 3

738. _____ - 11 = 78

739. 98 - 44 = _____

740. _____ - 29 = 69

741. _____ - 53 = 19

742. 49 - _____ = 21

743. _____ - 63 = 10

744. 95 - 14 = _____

745. 56 - _____ = 43

746. _____ - 22 = 45

747. _____ - 4 = 18

748. 79 - 40 = _____

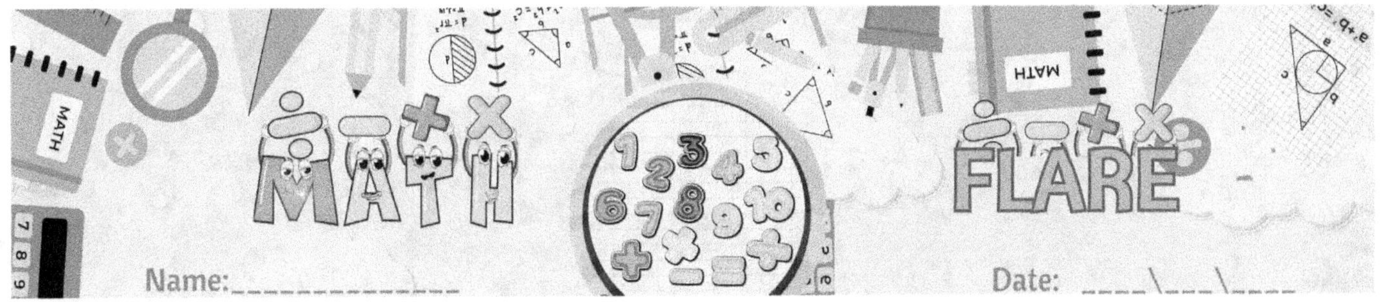

749. _____ - 34 = 28

750. 24 - 4 = _____

751. 61 - _____ = 57

752. _____ - 38 = 0

753. 61 - 13 = _____

754. _____ - 19 = 80

755. 88 - _____ = 10

756. 32 - _____ = 24

757. _____ - 43 = 23

758. 100 - 57 = _____

759. 59 - 19 = _____

760. _____ - 17 = 14

761. _____ - 2 = 9

762. 82 - 10 = _____

763. 58 - 34 = _____

764. 31 - 12 = _____

765. 26 - _____ = 16

766. 58 - _____ = 32

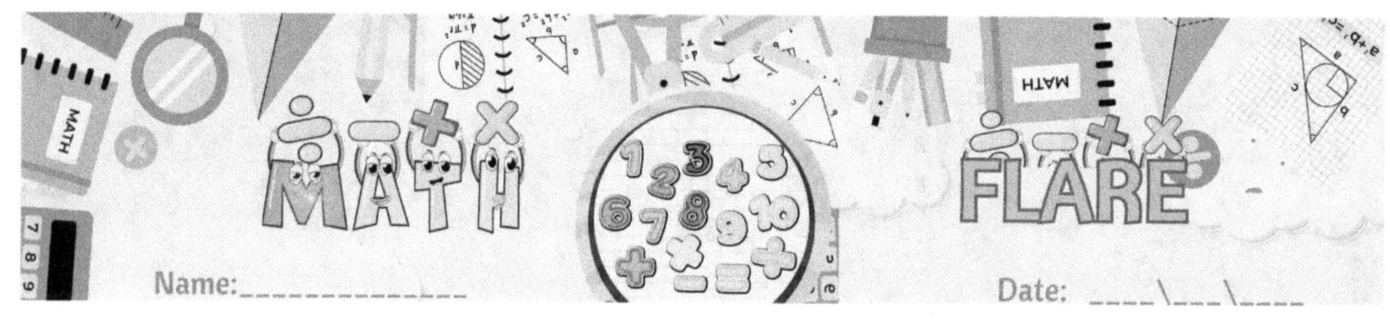

767. 36 - ____ = 5

768. ____ - 48 = 27

769. 48 - ____ = 26

770. 11 - ____ = 5

771. 89 - ____ = 21

772. ____ - 22 = 13

773. 98 - ____ = 59

774. 72 - ____ = 37

775. 24 - 6 = ____

776. 97 - 26 = ____

777. 37 - 24 = ____

778. ____ - 10 = 11

779. 32 - ____ = 25

780. ____ - 51 = 1

781. 97 - ____ = 38

782. 10 - ____ = 5

783. ____ - 34 = 8

784. ____ - 74 = 21

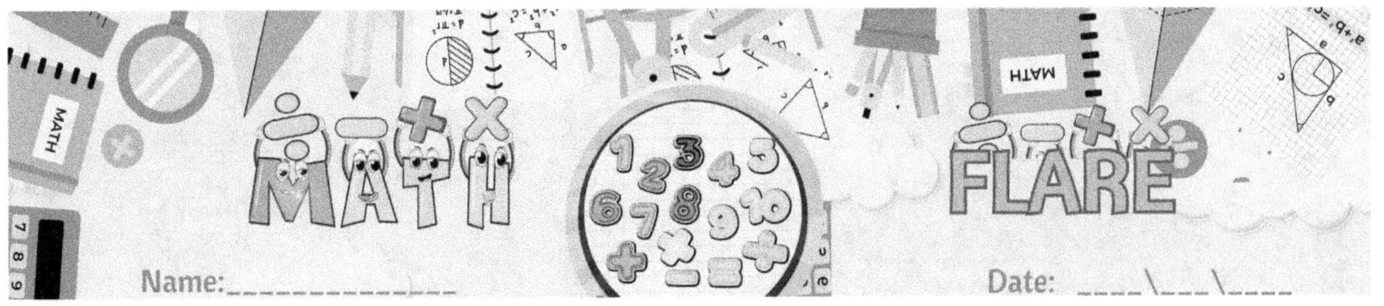

785. 93 - ____ = 59

786. 23 - 3 = ____

787. 38 - ____ = 10

788. ____ - 18 = 50

789. 86 - ____ = 70

790. 90 - ____ = 23

791. ____ - 30 = 1

792. 48 - ____ = 34

793. 22 - ____ = 7

794. 75 - 22 = ____

795. ____ - 11 = 35

796. ____ - 3 = 95

797. 59 - ____ = 42

798. 78 - ____ = 15

799. 34 - ____ = 27

800. ____ - 47 = 4

801. 60 - ____ = 12

802. 15 - 13 = ____

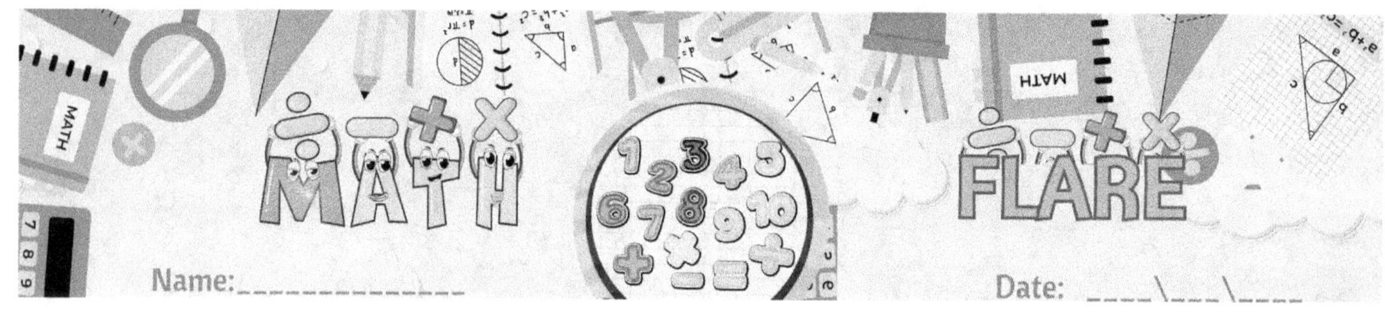

Addition Word Problems

803. Emilia has 4 sticks. Her friend gives her 9 more sticks. How many sticks does Emilia have now?

804. A basket holds 9 calendars. If 6 more calendars are added to the basket, how many calendars will the basket hold in total?

805. Tristan spent 8 hours studying for the history exam on Monday and 10 hours studying for the science exam on Tuesday. How many hours did Tristan spend studying in total?

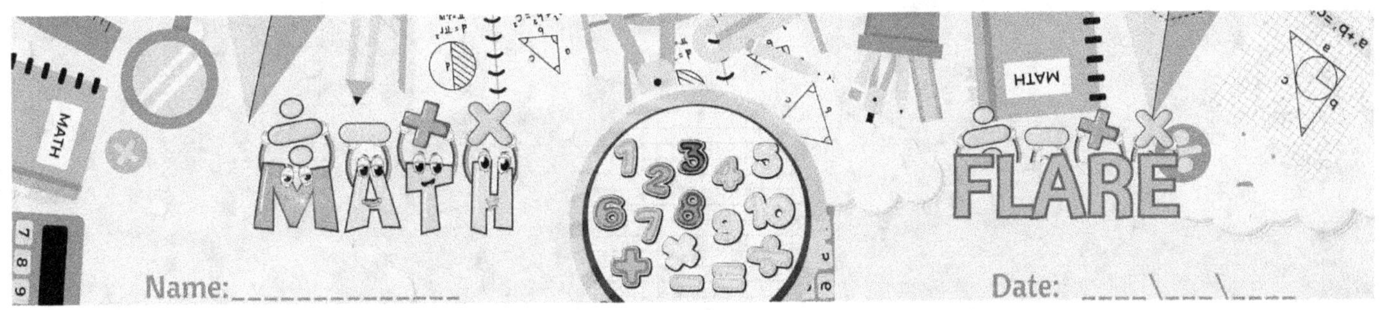

806. There are 5 cats in the ground. 10 more cats come to play. How many cats are in the ground now?

807. Emmett made 10 cookies and Emma made 7 cookies. How many cookies were made in total?

808. The weight of an empty container is 6 pounds. If the container is filled with 9 pounds of shirts, what is the total weight of the container and its contents?

809. Sebastian has 1 scarf. He buys 8 more scarves. How many scarves does she have now?

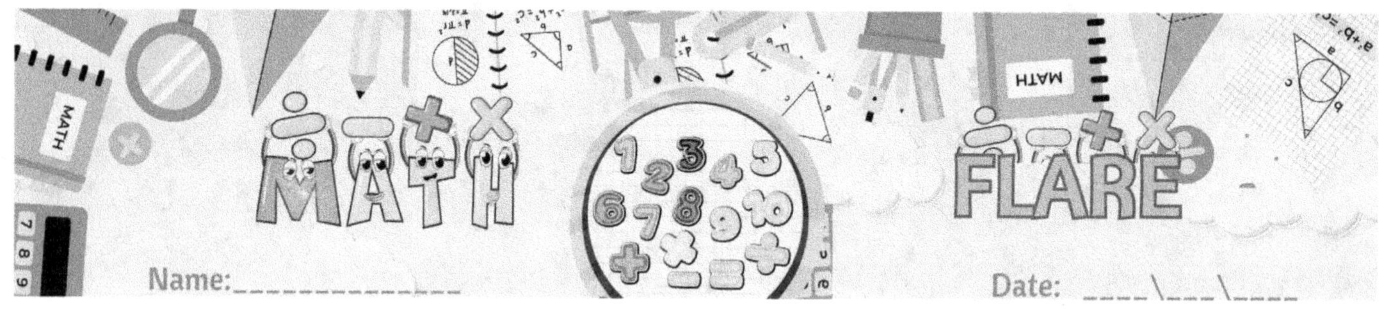

810. There are 5 fishes in the pond. 1 more fishes join them. How many fishes are in the pond now?

811. Yesterday, Reagan earned $6, and today, Reagan earned $9. How much money did Reagan earn in total?

812. Noah drove 8 miles in the morning and 5 miles in the evening. How many miles did Noah drive in total?

813. James has 1 phone. His sister gives him 6 more phones . How many phones does James have now?

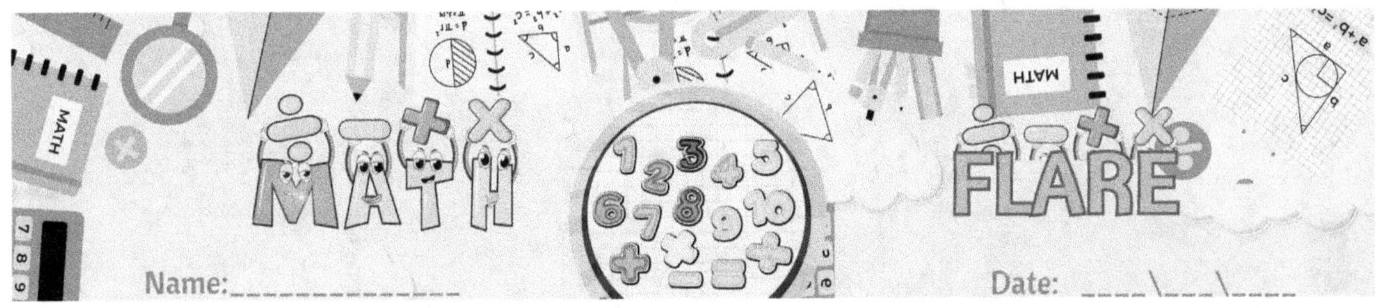

814. Kai has 3 chocolates and buys 3 more chocolates. How many chocolates does Kai have in total?

815. There is 1 kids playing on the playground. 8 more kids join them. How many kids are playing now?

816. Bella bought 10 mirrors and later bought 7 mirrors. How many mirrors does Bella have now?

817. Asher has 3 scalpels. He finds 10 more scalpels on the ground. How many scalpels does Asher have now?

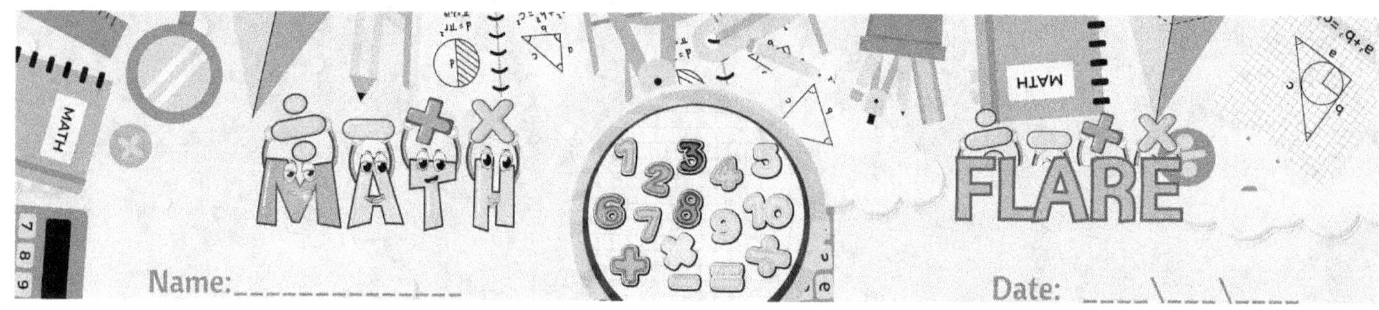

818. Michael has 6 apples and 5 oranges in a basket. How many fruits does Michael have in total?

819. Justin has 2 scrubs. He gets 8 more scrubs. How many scrubs does he have now?

820. At the start of the school year, there were 4 students enrolled in English class. By the end of the year, 2 more students had enrolled. How many students were enrolled in English class at the end of the year?

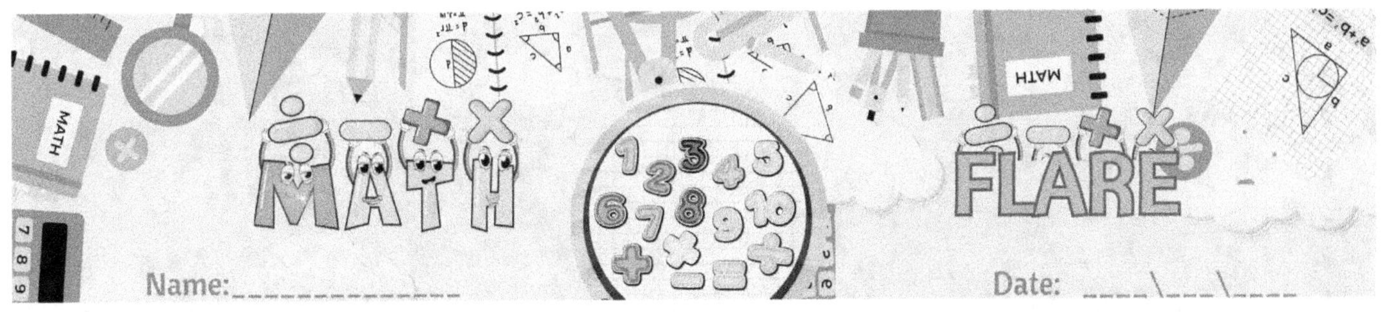

821. Aria bought pizzas with 10 slices. Later, Aria bought some more pizzas with 2 slices. How many slices of pizzas does Aria have in total?

822. Daniel has 3 red cups and 5 green cups. If Daniel puts all the cups in a basket, how many cups are in the basket in total?

823. At the beginning of the week, there were 9 perfumes in the bag. By the end of the week, 5 more perfumes were added to the bag. How many perfumes are in the bag now?

824. Camila has 1 thermometer. She buys 9 more thermometers at the store. How many thermometers does Camila have now?

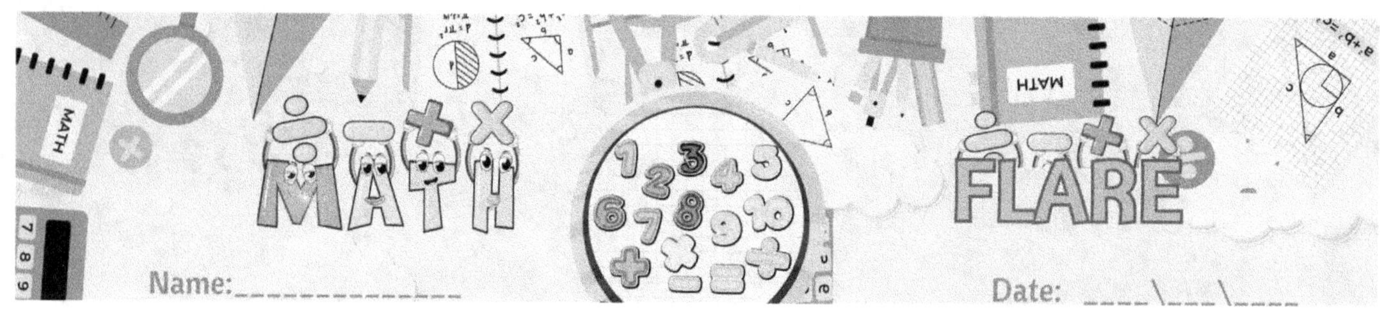

825. A soccer team scored 7 goals in the first half and 7 goals in the second half. What was the total score of the soccer team?

826. At the beginning of the week, there were 2 apples in the basket. By the end of the week, 3 more apples were added to the basket. How many apples are in the basket now?

827. Caroline sold 9 bananas on Monday and 5 bananas on Tuesday. How many bananas did the she sell in total?

828. At the start of the week, 3 tissues were in the store. By the end of the week, 6 more tissues were added to the store. How many tissues are in the store now?

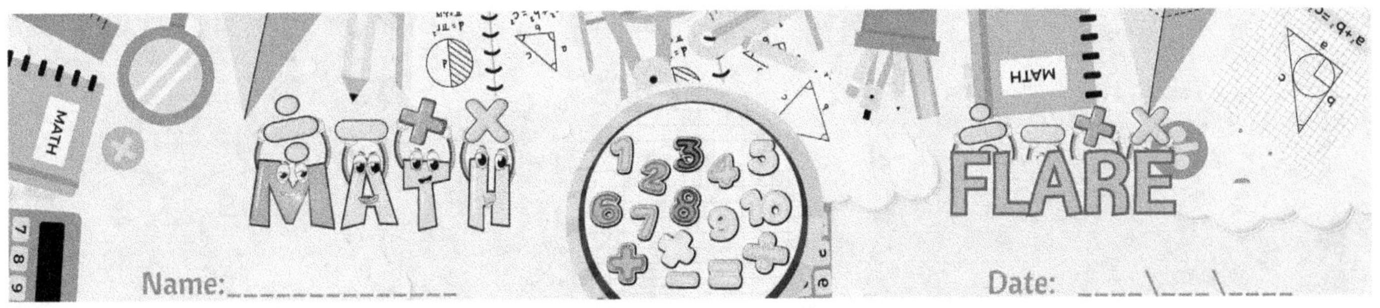

829. Madison has 3 dresses. She gets 4 more dresses. How many dresses does Madison have now?

830. Avery walked 9 miles yesterday and 9 miles today. How many miles did Avery walk in total?

831. Cooper has 6 cameras. He receives 7 more cameras. How many cameras does he have now?

832. Lydia watched 5 movies last week and 10 movies this week. How many movies did Lydia watch altogether?

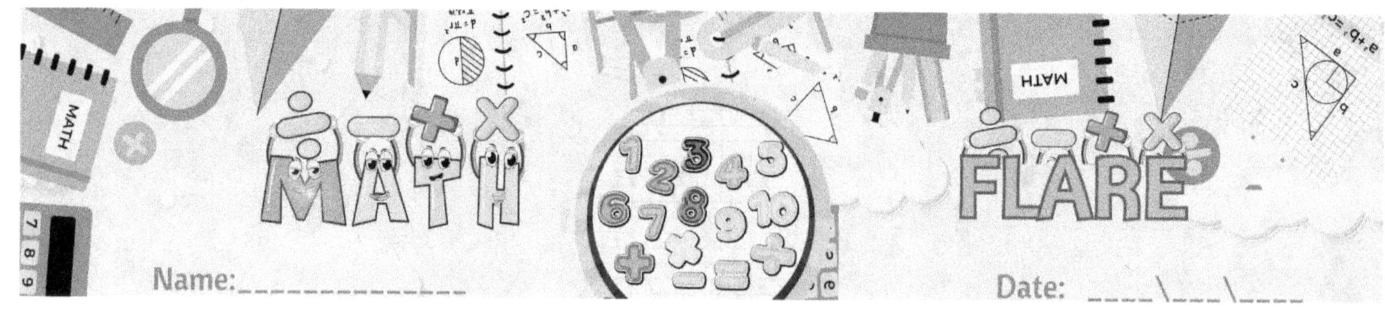

Subtraction Word Problems

833. Claire had 8 dollars. She spent 8 dollars on phones. How much money does Claire have left?

834. Adalyn bought globes for 3 dollars. She later returned some globes and received a refund of 3 dollars. How much money did she end up spending on globes?

835. Aurora has 1 stick in her collection. She gave 1 of them to her friend. How many sticks does Aurora have now?

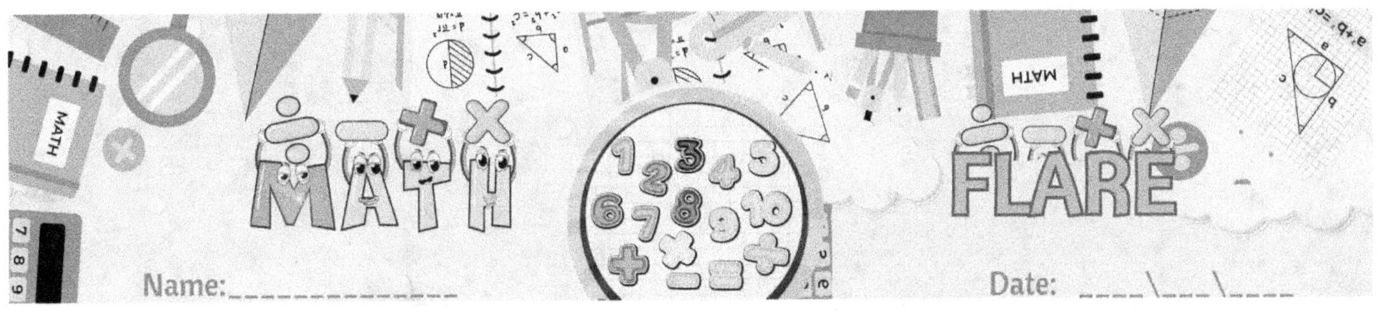

836. Luke has 3 dollars. He wants to buy forks that costs 1 dollars. How much more money does he need to buy the forks?

837. If scarves costs 8 dollars and you have 6 dollars, how much more money do you need to buy it?

838. There were 2 students in a class. 2 of them were absent. How many students were present in the class?

839. Arianna has 3 combs. She lost 3 of them. How many combs does Arianna have left?

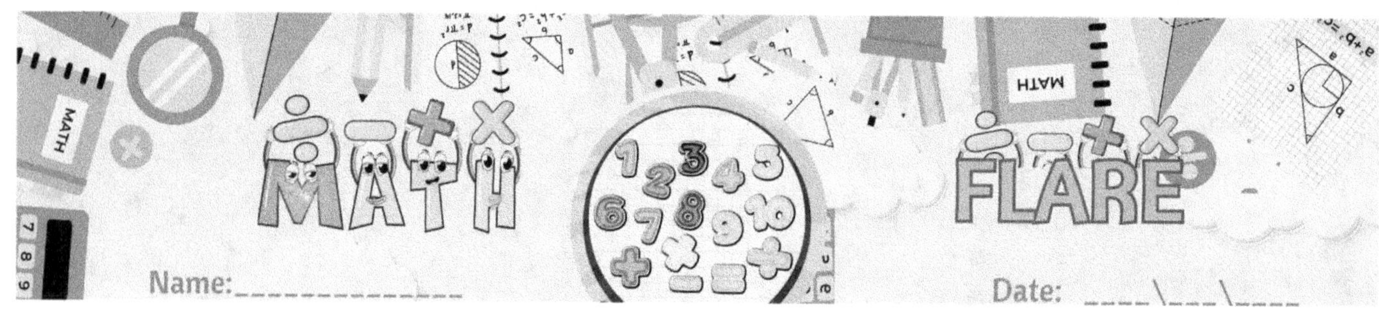

840. There is 1 dogs in a park. If 1 leave, how many dogs are left in the park?

841. Hailey bought stethoscopes for 2 dollars. She received 1 dollars in change. How much did stethoscopes cost?

842. A pack of gum had 7 pieces. Savannah took 7 pieces of gum. How many pieces of gum are left in the pack?

843. Amelia and Aubrey had 1 bat altogether. Aubrey gave 1 bat to Jaxon. How many bats do they have left?

844. Miles has 3 dollars. He needs to buy vitamins that costs 8 dollars. How much money will he have left after buying the vitamins?

845. Gauzes originally cost 7 dollars, but it is now on sale for 2 dollars. How much money can you save by buying it on sale?

846. There are 10 syringes in a bag. Lily took 1 syringe out of the bag. How many syringes are still in the bag?

847. Nicholas is 1 years old and Landon is 1 years old. What is the difference in their ages?

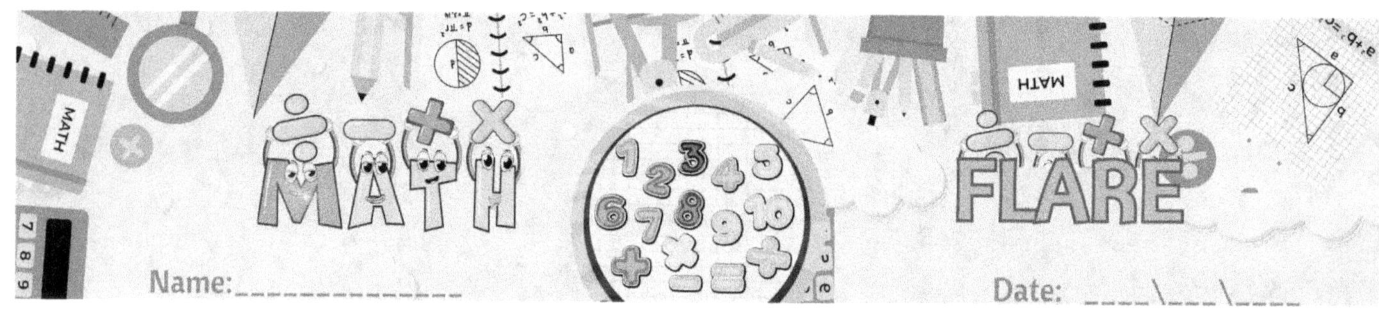

848. There are 10 cars in a parking lot. Ryan took 7 cars out of the lot. How many cars are still in the lot?

849. There are 3 fish in a tank. If 3 leave, how many fish are left in the tank?

850. If you have 5 muffins and you give away 3, how many muffins do you have left?

851. Audrey baked a 5 cookies. 5 of them were chocolate chip cookies and the rest were oatmeal raisin cookies. How many oatmeal raisin cookies did Audrey bake?

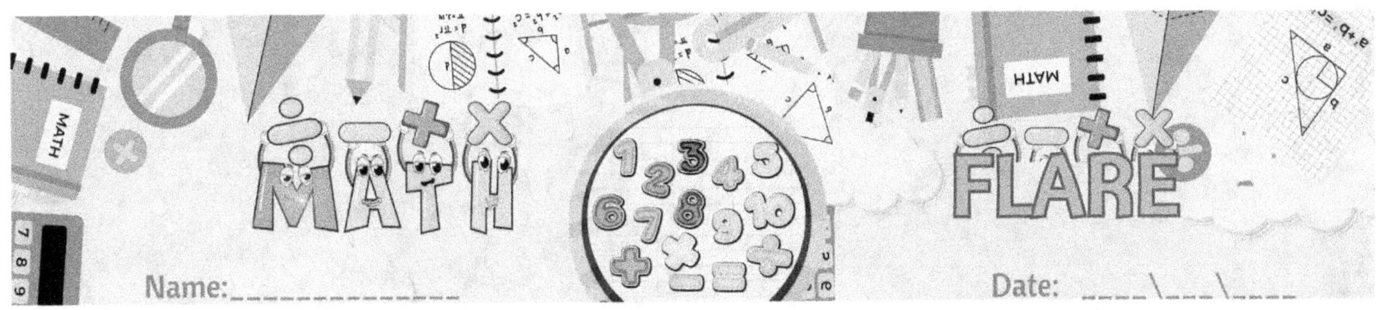

852. A pizza has 10 slices. Aria ate 2 slices. How many slices of pizza are left?

853. A small bag of chips has 7 chips in it. Elijah ate 4 chips. How many chips are left in the bag?

854. There are 7 flowers. 6 flowers are blue and the rest are red. How many red flowers are in the box?

855. A cake recipe calls for 6 cups of flour. 6 cups of flour have already been added. How many more cups of flour are needed?

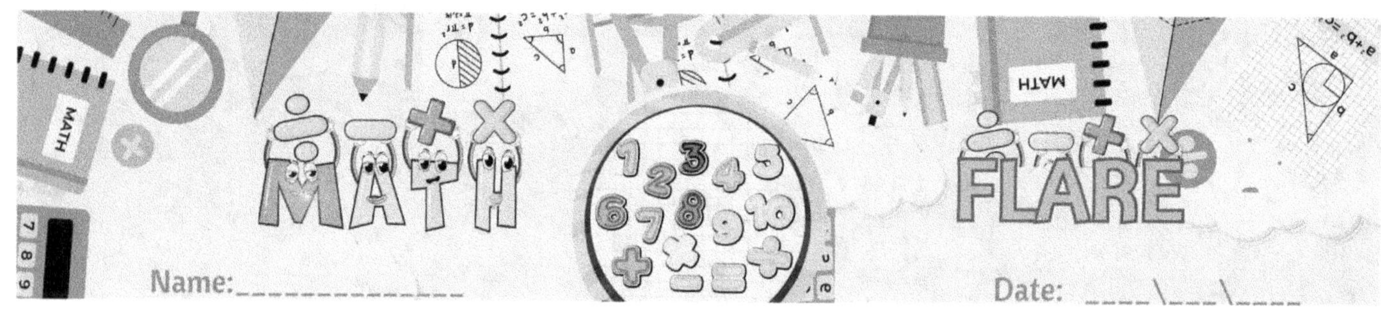

856. A box of tissues weighs 4 pounds. If you remove 1 pounds from it, how much does it weigh now?

857. A recipe needs 8 cups of sugar. Elizabeth added 5 cups of sugar. How many cups of sugar are still needed?

858. Mason has 7 medicines in his collection. He sold 4 of them at a sale. How many medicines does he have left in his collection?

859. There are 6 turtles in a pond. If 6 leave, how many turtles are left in the pond?

860. Jackson has 8 thermometers. He traded 6 of them with his friend. How many thermometers does Jackson have now?

861. Reagan and Jordyn went on a shopping spree and bought 2 lotions. After returning home, they realized that they didn't need 1 of them. How many lotions did they end up keeping?

862. Valentina has 2 dollars. She wants to buy tables, which costs 2 dollars. How much more money does she need to buy it?

863. Camila has 4 scalpels. She gave 2 scalpels to Naomi. How many scalpels does Camila have now?

ANSWERS

Page 1: Addition: 1 through 100

1. 100	2. 118	3. 119	4. 11	5. 128	6. 137	7. 163
8. 44	9. 77	10. 80	11. 149	12. 56	13. 79	14. 60
15. 94	16. 104	17. 119	18. 85	19. 48	20. 41	21. 105
22. 174	23. 96	24. 140	25. 102	26. 107	27. 125	28. 111
29. 128	30. 62	31. 109	32. 70	33. 120	34. 50	35. 110
36. 19	37. 75	38. 90	39. 92	40. 128	41. 122	42. 158
43. 73	44. 89	45. 115	46. 120	47. 92	48. 90	49. 157
50. 124	51. 151	52. 102	53. 127	54. 101	55. 111	56. 47
57. 168	58. 39	59. 95	60. 78	61. 138	62. 125	63. 176
64. 134	65. 96	66. 167	67. 89	68. 129	69. 51	70. 125
71. 32	72. 110	73. 104	74. 85	75. 143	76. 62	77. 49
78. 35	79. 78	80. 132	81. 150	82. 146	83. 120	84. 128
85. 53	86. 109	87. 95	88. 61	89. 121	90. 58	91. 84
92. 151	93. 176	94. 118	95. 124	96. 143	97. 121	98. 141
99. 101	100. 10	101. 78	102. 60	103. 123	104. 145	105. 175
106. 103	107. 84	108. 78	109. 158	110. 101	111. 162	112. 189
113. 78	114. 123	115. 148	116. 93			

Page 7: Subtraction: 1 through 100

117. 45	118. 1	119. 16	120. 34	121. 12	122. 65	123. 47

124. 32   125. 46   126. 17   127. 1   128. 15   129. 52   130. 43

131. 52   132. 67   133. 14   134. 71   135. 30   136. 33   137. 9

138. 1   139. 3   140. 27   141. 3   142. 46   143. 12   144. 33

145. 6   146. 34   147. 38   148. 26   149. 54   150. 62   151. 52

152. 44   153. 35   154. 72   155. 67   156. 8   157. 19   158. 1

159. 26   160. 32   161. 43   162. 3   163. 61   164. 18   165. 28

166. 35   167. 9   168. 7   169. 6   170. 48   171. 3   172. 11

173. 19   174. 4   175. 5   176. 16   177. 5   178. 55   179. 1

180. 19   181. 2   182. 34   183. 10   184. 85   185. 10   186. 18

187. 68   188. 9   189. 39   190. 22   191. 37   192. 51   193. 50

194. 9   195. 26   196. 37   197. 20   198. 22   199. 1   200. 46

201. 4   202. 9   203. 42   204. 9   205. 9   206. 5   207. 83

208. 5   209. 5   210. 0   211. 16   212. 17   213. 77   214. 40

215. 15   216. 61   217. 8   218. 25   219. 18   220. 15   221. 3

222. 39   223. 38   224. 21   225. 26   226. 8   227. 48   228. 29

229. 87   230. 10   231. 19   232. 8

Page 13: Addition with Regrouping

233. 180   234. 125   235. 160   236. 111   237. 31   238. 171

239. 111   240. 113   241. 131   242. 133   243. 30   244. 50

245. 133   246. 113   247. 110   248. 61   249. 150   250. 50

251. 40   252. 132   253. 160   254. 116   255. 172   256. 114

257. 137   258. 130   259. 141   260. 135   261. 147   262. 123

263. 170   264. 111   265. 110   266. 164   267. 176   268. 50

269. 65   270. 120   271. 110   272. 112   273. 125   274. 132

275. 111   276. 121   277. 143   278. 141   279. 110   280. 40

281. 145   282. 71   283. 141   284. 80   285. 131   286. 130

287. 141   288. 130   289. 112   290. 126   291. 111   292. 20

293. 111   294. 120   295. 130   296. 92   297. 113   298. 123

299. 110   300. 170   301. 170   302. 121   303. 120   304. 184

305. 30   306. 93   307. 120   308. 150   309. 138   310. 120

311. 113   312. 121   313. 150   314. 110   315. 141   316. 140

317. 122   318. 110   319. 110   320. 140   321. 111   322. 65

323. 125   324. 110   325. 30   326. 110   327. 151   328. 64

329. 67   330. 120   331. 121   332. 111   333. 150   334. 116

335. 122   336. 140   337. 167   338. 124   339. 173   340. 112

341. 115   342. 154   343. 113   344. 113   345. 156   346. 131

347. 135   348. 143   349. 103   350. 132   351. 143   352. 110

Page 19: Subtraction with Regrouping

353. 11   354. 26   355. 8   356. 8   357. 73   358. 13   359. 3

360. 31   361. 4   362. 29   363. 15   364. 17   365. 13   366. 6

367. 17   368. 4   369. 3   370. 13   371. 31   372. 13   373. 3

374. 14   375. 48   376. 3   377. 8   378. 5   379. 3   380. 7

381. 37   382. 13   383. 28   384. 16   385. 18   386. 24   387. 9

388. 1   389. 5   390. 6   391. 4   392. 0   393. 12   394. 22

395. 26   396. 67   397. 21   398. 11   399. 35   400. 9   401. 9

402. 23   403. 0   404. 38   405. 25   406. 68   407. 34   408. 77

409. 52   410. 27   411. 21   412. 28   413. 3   414. 3   415. 33

416. 15   417. 19   418. 62   419. 4   420. 34   421. 25   422. 1

423. 59   424. 7   425. 35   426. 31   427. 25   428. 18   429. 16

430. 5   431. 28   432. 27   433. 22   434. 39   435. 45   436. 6

437. 35   438. 28   439. 33   440. 35   441. 41   442. 32   443. 21

444. 51   445. 28   446. 62   447. 5   448. 15   449. 15   450. 85

451. 81   452. 23   453. 37   454. 7   455. 49   456. 4   457. 64

458. 5   459. 12   460. 56   461. 36   462. 6   463. 24   464. 37

465. 58   466. 12   467. 2   468. 31

Page 25: Make 100

469. 70   470. 89   471. 49   472. 54   473. 76   474. 58   475. 31

476. 59   477. 5   478. 80   479. 30   480. 55   481. 72   482. 81

483. 98   484. 79   485. 90   486. 96   487. 7   488. 84   489. 3

490. 56   491. 23   492. 93   493. 38   494. 37   495. 36   496. 40

497. 45   498. 43   499. 21   500. 51   501. 91   502. 4   503. 78

504. 33   505. 52   506. 39   507. 20   508. 0   509. 27   510. 17

511. 65   512. 94   513. 75   514. 71   515. 87   516. 2   517. 15

518. 73

Page 28: Addition: Unknown Number

519. 24	520. 23	521. 87	522. 167	523. 70	524. 111
525. 99	526. 60	527. 18	528. 84	529. 24	530. 105
531. 59	532. 30	533. 20	534. 20	535. 36	536. 190
537. 112	538. 85	539. 108	540. 32	541. 13	542. 65
543. 104	544. 2	545. 84	546. 10	547. 142	548. 28
549. 70	550. 77	551. 27	552. 63	553. 10	554. 53
555. 40	556. 90	557. 13	558. 49	559. 79	560. 119
561. 19	562. 63	563. 117	564. 12	565. 55	566. 85
567. 77	568. 18	569. 136	570. 117	571. 67	572. 69
573. 35	574. 22	575. 14	576. 161	577. 7	578. 91
579. 70	580. 26	581. 47	582. 79	583. 60	584. 92
585. 37	586. 116	587. 127	588. 97	589. 86	590. 97
591. 49	592. 84	593. 68	594. 79	595. 16	596. 83
597. 20	598. 29	599. 140	600. 40	601. 41	602. 62
603. 87	604. 60	605. 80	606. 120	607. 71	608. 64
609. 43	610. 7	611. 96	612. 67	613. 77	614. 97
615. 71	616. 5	617. 76	618. 78	619. 87	620. 85
621. 62	622. 75	623. 40	624. 86	625. 53	626. 29
627. 102	628. 71	629. 127	630. 6	631. 34	632. 67

633. 34 634. 2 635. 79 636. 34 637. 113 638. 96
639. 153 640. 67 641. 150 642. 101 643. 119 644. 75
645. 50 646. 49 647. 98 648. 6 649. 72 650. 45
651. 45 652. 8 653. 20 654. 63 655. 52 656. 84
657. 122 658. 90 659. 26 660. 125

Page 36: Subtraction: Unknown Number

661. 31 662. 7 663. 93 664. 11 665. 54 666. 3 667. 36
668. 9 669. 36 670. 8 671. 44 672. 11 673. 6 674. 45
675. 44 676. 11 677. 86 678. 25 679. 11 680. 27 681. 9
682. 22 683. 40 684. 20 685. 23 686. 44 687. 14 688. 24
689. 28 690. 9 691. 30 692. 3 693. 98 694. 21 695. 4
696. 14 697. 33 698. 81 699. 17 700. 32 701. 14 702. 19
703. 22 704. 71 705. 25 706. 56 707. 3 708. 63 709. 10
710. 18 711. 11 712. 33 713. 8 714. 21 715. 17 716. 8
717. 4 718. 16 719. 85 720. 79 721. 53 722. 24 723. 18
724. 42 725. 11 726. 29 727. 17 728. 22 729. 28 730. 30
731. 37 732. 85 733. 45 734. 34 735. 32 736. 33 737. 58
738. 89 739. 54 740. 98 741. 72 742. 28 743. 73 744. 81
745. 13 746. 67 747. 22 748. 39 749. 62 750. 20 751. 4
752. 38 753. 48 754. 99 755. 78 756. 8 757. 66 758. 43
759. 40 760. 31 761. 11 762. 72 763. 24 764. 19 765. 10

766. 26   767. 31   768. 75   769. 22   770. 6   771. 68   772. 35

773. 39   774. 35   775. 18   776. 71   777. 13   778. 21   779. 7

780. 52   781. 59   782. 5   783. 42   784. 95   785. 34   786. 20

787. 28   788. 68   789. 16   790. 67   791. 31   792. 14   793. 15

794. 53   795. 46   796. 98   797. 17   798. 63   799. 7   800. 51

801. 48   802. 2

Page 44: Addition Word Problems

803. 13   804. 15   805. 18   806. 15   807. 17   808. 15   809. 9   810. 6

811. 15   812. 13   813. 7   814. 6   815. 9   816. 17   817. 13   818. 11

819. 10   820. 6   821. 12   822. 8   823. 14   824. 10   825. 14   826. 5

827. 14   828. 9   829. 7   830. 18   831. 13   832. 15

Page 52: Subtraction Word Problems

833. 0   834. 0   835. 0   836. 2   837. 2   838. 0   839. 0   840. 0

841. 1   842. 0   843. 0   844. 5   845. 5   846. 9   847. 0   848. 3

849. 0   850. 2   851. 0   852. 8   853. 3   854. 1   855. 0   856. 3

857. 3   858. 3   859. 0   860. 2   861. 1   862. 0   863. 2

9 798869 372093